The Legendary
BRUCE LEE

by THE EDITORS
of BLACK BELT MAGAZINE

ELISHA D. SMITH PUBLIC LIBRARY
MENASHA, WISCONSIN

Compiled by Jack Vaughn and Mike Lee
Graphic Design: Karen Massad
Art Production: Katherine Arion
Photos courtesy of Black Belt, Karate Illustrated, and Fighting Stars magazines.

©1986 Ohara Publications, Inc.
All rights reserved
Printed in the United States of America
Library of Congress Catalog Card Number: 86-42770
ISBN 0-89750-106-3

Fourteenth printing 2000

WARNING

OHARA PUBLICATIONS, INCORPORATED
SANTA CLARITA, CALIFORNIA

Introduction

Everyone who knew him agreed that Bruce Lee had a certain chemistry. He was a catalyst. Those who have written about him, for instance, all have used very plain language because he had evoked in them that old desire for simplicity, economy, and straightforwardness, the important tenets of his style.

Bruce Lee, the Man, the Fighter, the Superstar by M. Uyehara starts off this book as part one because it is a general, yet thorough, biography of Bruce Lee which tells the story from his formative years in Hong Kong to his rise as an actor and maturity as a martial artist.

Part two is about his martial art. The general public first became aware of Bruce Lee's art through the television series *The Green Hornet* which also launched his acting career in the U.S. Maxwell Pollard's two articles, based on interviews with Lee during and immediately following the series, centers on the reality behind the illusion. The first, through interviews, explores Bruce's martial art. In the second, the author is given a personal lesson in the principles of jeet kune do as Lee explains it during a workout in his Chinatown school.

Lee's Spartan life-style and rigorous daily training are detailed in Mitch Stom's article *Bruce Lee's Training Methods.* Stom goes into depth to show the extraordinary exercises and gym equipment Lee developed to condition his body.

To conclude the second part, the article *Liberate Yourself from Classical Karate* written by Bruce Lee is included. Here, Lee summarizes his philosophy as it has influenced his martial art. Lee, the pragmatist, pushes toward explaining the essence of jeet kune do, and comes as close as he ever did to describing a whole way of life.

Part three covers Lee's work in the movies. *Super Star Bruce Lee, An Acclaimed Phenomenon* by Mike Plane gives an overview of Bruce's movie career. After that, *Date with Destiny,* by the same author, tells of Bruce's collaboration with Raymond Chow and Lo Wei. Next, Linda Lee's account of the making of *Way of the Dragon,* a film which Lee directed himself, is followed by Steve Jacques' article on the making of *Enter the Dragon,* Bruce's biggest Hollywood film.

Part four consists of reminiscenses by friends including students, fellow martial artists, movie executives, and celebrities. All give their personal impressions of Bruce Lee and tell of their involvement with him.

Contents

PART 1

Chapter 1

Bruce Lee
The Man, the Fighter,
the Superstar

by M. Uyehara

He died a thousand times. Year after year, death haunted Bruce Lee, until the fatal day of July 20, 1973, when he finally met death at the young age of 32.

Since reaching fame from the television series *The Green Hornet,* in which he played Kato, Bruce's name was always associated with fighting and death. Rumors were constantly being circulated that he was always fighting ten or more assailants and that he had either been wounded or killed after he had slain three or more punks.

"One day, I got a long-distance call from Hong Kong's largest newspaper," explained Lee. "They asked me if I was still alive. 'Guess who you're talking to?' I replied. 'Nope, I haven't gotten into a fight.'

" 'But it's headlined in all the newspapers here that you were killed by some ruffians,' the dumbfounded reporter told me."

Besides rumors of death, Bruce was also haunted by stories of someone beating him up. Bruce had made enemies on both continents, and they apparently used his name to enhance their ego and fame. Perhaps their resentment was a reaction to his seemingly conceited attitude when he arrived in the United States for the first time. "Yeah, Bruce was real cocky when I first met him," said Leo Fong, then a Methodist minister, "but he simmered down quite a bit as he matured."

Bruce feared no man. He had so much confidence in his ability that he dared not back off from any challenge. "While I was a student at the university (University of Washington, Seattle)," Bruce once recalled, "I gave a demonstration of kung fu. While explaining the art is the forerunner of karate, I was rudely interrupted by a black belt karateman from Japan who sat in front of the stage.

"'No, no, karate not from China. Come from Japan!' he hollered."

Bruce reiterated superciliously, "Karate is from kung fu."

After the crowd left, the karateman challenged Bruce. "You want to fight?"

"Anytime," Bruce retorted.

"OK, I fight you next week."

"Why not now?" asked Bruce.

The Lee family poses for a portrait in Hong Kong without the father. Members of the family include from left to right, Peter Lee, Agnes Lee Chan, Phoebe Lee Ho, and Bruce Lee. Robert sits with his mother on the bottom row.

"It only took me two seconds to dispose of him," Bruce recalled. "He was too slow and too stiff."

In 1967, BLACK BELT magazine interviewed Bruce. By that time, he had already converted his fighting style from wing chun to *jeet kune do* (literally, the way of the intercepting fist).

"I saw the limitation in wing chun," Bruce explained. "I'd gotten into a fight in San Francisco with a kung fu cat, and after a brief encounter the son-of-a-bitch started to run. I chased him and, like a fool, kept punching him behind his head and back. Soon my fists began to swell from hitting his hard head. Right then I realized wing chun was not too practical and began to alter my way of fighting."

Bruce's outspoken ways made even more enemies. In his interview with BLACK BELT, Bruce blasted the Chinese classical kung fu practitioners and other martial artists for practicing *kata* (forms). "What a waste of time!" he chastised. "How can you fight by doing kata? There's no way a person is going to fight you in the street with a set pattern."

The Challenge

The challenges began to roll in. One kung fu instructor scurrilously attacked Bruce, saying that the young man didn't know enough to make such

Bruce Lee in his first starring role, in the 1958 film, The Orphan, *made in Hong Kong. The first phase of his film career was as a child actor; the second followed his role as* The Green Hornet's *Kato on American television.*

The classic Bruce Lee side kick (top) took years to perfect. Early photos (above) of Lee taken in Hong Kong show how the budding star looked before working in various Cantonese films. The Lee qualities were already apparent as a teenager (right).

criticisms. A few days later, Bruce decided to meet the instructor and challenged him to a sparring match. When the instructor retorted that he didn't spar and would only use his art in a life-and-death situation, Bruce unhesitantly responded, "OK, let's go somewhere right now and have it out." Bruce was not the type to be bluffed. He would spar or fight anyone, even an opponent twice his size.

Although Bruce was reared in Hong Kong, he was born in San Francisco on November 27, 1940. At the time, his dad, Hoi Chuen Lee, a Chinese opera singer, was traveling on the East Coast, while his mother, Grace, remained on the West Coast with friends to await the arrival of her fourth baby, Bruce. The child was named Jun Fan (which means ever or always San Francisco) by his parents, but his anglicized name, Bruce, was given to him by the doctor who delivered him.

After five months, Bruce and his parents returned to Hong Kong, but not before he had already made his presence known in movies. He was a baby "stand-in" in *Golden Gate Girl,* an American production.

When the family reached Hong Kong, the hot and humid weather affected Bruce. He soon became very sick and weak, and his mother had to constantly look after him. But as he regained his health, he became robust and effervescent, which was to become a life-long characteristic.

When he was among friends or associates, Bruce dominated the spotlight, continuously gesticulating and hopping among the group. He could not remain still for a second, a trait which became a problem when he severely hurt his back in 1970 while improperly training with heavy weights.

From childhood to fatherhood, streetfighter to artist, from years of trying to final success, the disparate aspects of Bruce's life, seemingly held together into a functioning whole by sheer self-confidence, are well documented by photos such as this taken with his two children, Brandon and Shannon.

Bruce Lee's varied life can be seen in many photos taken at various periods. Here (clockwise from the top) Lee the child-actor in one of his early Hong Kong films; the University of Washington where he studied after leaving Hong Kong; practicing a dance routine during his reign as the Hong Kong cha-cha champion; and Lee posing in 1963 with his father and youngest brother Robert, who eventually became a popular folk singer in Hong Kong.

Before his death, Lee posed with his mother, Grace Lee, and his son Brandon in Hong Kong in 1970 (left). Another family portrait (above) shows Bruce as a baby with his father, Chinese opera singer Hoi Chuen Lee, and a youthful Grace Lee.

After his doctor examined him, Bruce was ordered to remain in bed. But he was restless and spent more time out of bed than in it. For a while, it seemed he would never recover from the injury.

When friends visited him, he became overly enthusiastic, throwing high kicks or hard punches and only quitting when he felt the pain in his back.

In his early teens, Bruce had to transfer from one parochial school to another, even though the teachers seemed to like him, says his mother. "But somehow Bruce regularly got into fights with other children." Long after Bruce left school, the legend of "Bruce, the bully and troublemaker" still continued.

Being a skinny kid, Bruce recalled, "I always fought with my gang behind me. In school, our favorite weapons were the chains we'd find in the 'cans.' Those days, kids improvised all kinds of weapons—even shoes with razors attached."

A City of Ghettos

To Bruce, Hong Kong seemed to be a city of ghettos, everyone trying to make a living and no one getting anywhere. To belong to a gang was a natural motivation among the youngsters. "I only took up kung fu," Bruce confided, "when I began to feel insecure. I kept wondering what would happen to me if my gang was not around when I met a rival gang."

According to Bruce's younger brother, Robert, Bruce had studied several

Bruce Lee's famous low kick, demonstrated here with Dan Lee, was the technique he felt was the most effective in streetfighting. In the wing chun system he studied, most kicks are low.

different styles of kung fu but chose wing chun. "Bruce felt it was the most effective style of kung fu then."

Bruce once mentioned that the Chinese *kwoon* (school) was not like the Japanese *dojo* (school). "I have to give the Japanese credit for installing regimentation in their schools," he said. "The Japanese *sensei* (instructor) is revered and his command is law; but not the kung fu instructor *(sifu)*. We used to address our instructor with, 'Hey, old man, what do you have in mind for us to do?' If we didn't like what he wanted us to do, we used to say, 'Goddamit! We have to do that crap again?' "

Bruce explained that many juvenile hoodlums and punks took up kung fu but didn't remain with it long. "They didn't take kung fu for health reasons but just to learn to fight," an attitude which was not difficult to understand since the senior students and even some of the instructors smoked opium.

From time to time, a real match would take place on the roof of a tall building. Usually, it was between students from two different styles of kung fu.

"Like the old tradition, one school would challenge another," Bruce remembered, "and a designated place and time would be set. On the day of reckoning, both schools would have their instructors and students to cheer their fighter. Impromptu rules would be established, but those rules would be so minimal that the fight would be just about 'all out.' Nobody really got hurt because the arts weren't that effective. Those guys would have torn shirts and bloody noses, but I never saw anybody really get hurt badly enough to be sent to the hospital."

These contests were not really grudge fights, Bruce explained, but contests to find out which was the superior style of kung fu. After the battle, the fighters would shake hands and go to a restaurant for some tea.

Being a perfectionist, Bruce did not like defeat. While studying wing chun, he and other new students were often tormented by some of the older students during *chi sao* (sticking hands) practice. "Those bastards enjoyed overpowering us, and as we weakened they used to slap us on our chest and face. I got so mad one day that I decided to dish out the same medicine to them. I made a concentrated effort to develop my flowing energy. While attending class (high school), I began to press my arm at the edge of the desk and flowed my energy. (Martial artists usually refer to this inner energy as *chi* or *ki*.) One of the friendlier senior students spent some time after workouts exercising with me. In a few months, I got my revenge, and did I dish it out to them! I really picked on them after that."

In the Ring

During his senior year in high school, Bruce entered an amateur boxing contest. "I hadn't had any training in boxing," he admitted, "but decided to enter because I thought I was pretty good in wing chun and there wouldn't be much difference between my art and boxing. I never put on a glove before,

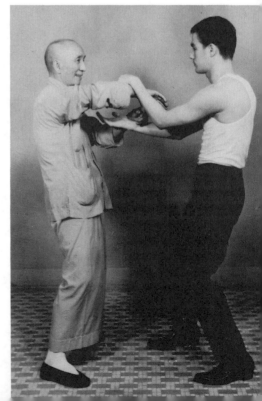

Lee and his wing chun teacher Yip Man (right) practice chi sao (sticky hands). Lee eventually became so good, he could do it blindfolded (above).

12

Bruce trained incessantly, always challenging himself and polishing his skills.

and it sure felt funny when I got into the ring. I learned to hit straightforward in wing chun, and that's what I did, knocking down my opponent." Bruce was declared the Hong Kong High School Champion, winning the High School cha cha championship the same year.

Bruce was always a slick dresser. "My parents weren't as poor as the rest of the population," he recalled. "They had several apartments in Hong Kong, and the rental income, plus my dad's income from his opera, brought in enough money that we always had two servants."

But it was his slick dressing which brought Bruce into a fight one night. "I was riding on this ferry late one night, and these two punks began to tease me. 'Are you a boy or a girl? You sure dress like a girl.' They kept taunting me, but I kept my cool and didn't say a word. As soon as the ferry docked, I followed them ashore and kind of baffled them when I began to cuss and swear at them. The bigger guy came after me, but I kicked him in his shin before he could do anything. While he was jumping up and down, hollering in pain, I went for the other guy, but he took off like a frightened rabbit."

At 18, Bruce starred in a Chinese movie called *The Orphan,* which became a big hit in Hong Kong and other parts of Asia. But by the time the movie was released, he was already in the United States. His dad had sent him abroad because he had never approved of Bruce being in movies, even though Bruce had appeared in motion pictures for many years. But the boy also had a bad temper, which led to constant fighting, and his father felt that in a new environment Bruce might change.

Like most Chinese fathers, Bruce's dad paid little attention to the children, spending most of his spare time in his private room reading. Nobody knows why Mr. Lee disapproved of his children's theatrical inclinations when he himself was in the profession. Nevertheless, both Bruce and his younger brother Robert became sensations in Hong Kong—Bruce as an actor and Robert as a singer.

Bruce was a believer in astrology. He returned to Hong Kong in 1963, after an absence of four years, and during his short stay he managed to see a fortune teller, who predicted that Bruce would not see his father again. On February 9, 1965, Bruce's dad passed away—before Bruce had a chance to return to Hong Kong again.

Even though Bruce's dad wasn't close to him, Bruce admired him and heeded some of his advice. "My dad use to tell me to save my dough because he knew I wanted to be an actor. He would say, 'When you become an actor, you can earn big money quickly, but when things are down, you may not see any money for months. So save everything you can to stretch your money when you need it.' "

The Lee Heritage

Bruce never mentioned it to his friends or to the media, but he had inherited a tint of German blood from his mother, who is three-fourths Chinese and one-fourth German. Bruce came from a family of five children. His brother Peter, a year older than Bruce, graduated from the University of Wisconsin in physics and is now a scientific officer at the Royal Observatory in Hong Kong. An adept fencer, Peter captured the Hong Kong championship in 1958 and participated in the Olympic trials in England.

Bruce didn't feel that it was unusual that his dad was closer to Peter than to himself. His older brother and father had similar characteristics—scholarly and reserved. Bruce, on the other hand, was always garrulous and, to some extent, a maverick.

When Bruce left Hong Kong for the United States, his dad was quite concerned about him. But Bruce made it on his own. "I never asked for any monetary help from my parents," he explained. "I just took any kind of job around. Like most Chinese kids who had just gotten off the boat, my first job

Working with Danny Inosanto in Los Angeles in the late 60s, Lee instructed the future jeet kune do instructor on the finer techniques of chi sao he had studied as a teenager under Yip Man.

was bussing and washing dishes in a restaurant.''

After a few months of kitchen duty at night and attending the University of Washington during the day, Bruce decided to teach kung fu. "I didn't really care about teaching kung fu, but it sure beat washing dishes!"

At that time, most kung fu practitioners trained in secret and only taught to Chinese. Bruce taught anyone he felt was worthy of learning the art. One of his school's instructors was Tak Kimura, who eventually became Bruce's instructor for the Seattle area.

Bruce's future wife, Linda, eventually joined his class, which led to their courtship and marriage. "Bruce attracted me right away by his action," Linda reminisces. "Somehow, he was able to enchant his audience. I guess it was his expression and his action. He was so lively and interesting. On campus, he always had a group of students following him."

Bruce's interests did not include too many sports, but he avidly followed boxing and all kinds of self-defense. He collected boxing films of Joe Louis, Max Baer, Muhammad Ali, and others. He also collected wrestling and martial arts books, paying as much as $400 for a rare book. As long as a book— good or bad—had something to do with self-defense he wanted it.

Whenever Bruce found a really exceptional martial arts book, he would read it over and over again, analyzing the techniques and finding the weaknesses. "Here's a counter for the overhead block," he would say, demonstrating the movement. Although he hadn't studied the other martial arts, like ka-

15

rate or judo, he could recite each karate and judo technique in Japanese and even demonstrate how it was done.

Bruce was an innovator—creative. He would constantly find ways to increase his power and speed in fighting. He created so much training equipment that he seldom needed a sparring partner. Actually, he spent more time working out alone in his garage (which had been converted into a gym) than with his students. Yet, he never lost his timing or speed when he sparred with his top students.

Not of Our Time

"Bruce was ahead of our time—at least 100 years," says Dan Inosanto, his protege—a rare accolade coming from one who has studied the martial arts for so many years (a black belt and eight years in kenpo karate and several years in kung fu and *escrima*, the Filipino martial art).

Jhoon Rhee, a top tae kwon do instructor in the U.S., agrees. "I don't know how Bruce did it. He moved in so fast, before you could even get set."

After converting his style of kung fu to jeet kune do, Bruce regretted ever having coined the term. "I hate to label any fighting into a style," he explained. "Fighting should not be stylized. When you fight, you should prepare to handle yourself against any kind of an opponent, whether he is a boxer, judoist, or wrestler."

Bruce combined several different sports in creating jeet kung do. For instance, he incorporated the southpaw stance from fencing. "The reason I took this unorthodox stance is because most of us are right-handed, and since the right hand and foot are faster and stronger than the left, why not

Although a physical fitness nut all his life, Bruce still found time to relax with his wife Linda every day. Bruce's sudden rise to fame created a more hectic professional life for him filled with martial arts and long hours of film work, but Linda kept things stable.

Lee's unique system of keeping fit included push-ups with his thumbs and two fingers (below). Also known for his iron-like forearms, which he developed through isometrics (right), Lee constantly trained by pushing against dead weight with his forearms.

utilize them by placing our right foot and right hand forward?" Bruce felt that this stance would allow the practitioner to utilize 80 percent of his right hand and foot.

Bruce was fast with his feet and hands—especially his hands. Back in the early 60s, he used to give demonstrations throughout the country. One of his favorite techniques was to ask a volunteer from the audience—usually a top karate player—to come up and block his punches. Most karate players expect to block a punch thrown to their face, especially if they are forewarned. But not one person was able to block Bruce's punches. Why? Just as a fencer does not signal his frontal attack, Bruce never telegraphed his punches. He was endowed with a keen awareness and was able to apply it in practice.

Bruce's boxing idol was Muhammad Ali, who was the greatest heavyweight boxer he had ever seen. Bruce used to watch Ali's films over and over again until he knew most of his movements. To adapt some of his

To develop his penetration techniques, Bruce used these square punching bags hung on the wall or the fence. They were filled with beans. The beans provided him with the feeling of hitting someone because they seemed to give way in a similar manner when struck with the same force and technique. Bruce also used other types of bags and fillings for other purposes.

techniques, Bruce would watch Ali's film through the reflection of a mirror. Since Bruce's stance was southpaw and Ali's is orthodox, he could view Ali's fighting in southpaw through the mirror.

After coming to the United States, Bruce became more conscious of his body and health. He began to eat nutritious food and did plenty of exercise. It was not unusual for him to gulp 1,500 milligrams of Vitamin C and run three miles a day on hilly roads. But Bruce did not go in for building big muscles. Instead, he exercised to develop plenty of small muscles and building power, which he could apply to his fighting. For instance, he had powerful abdominal muscles, to absorb blows to that area.

Bruce developed forearm muscles by lifting a 70-pound barbell straight out, holding it for a few seconds horizontally aligned with his chest. "Not many weightlifters can hold it that long," he used to say with pride. Sometimes he would sit on his couch watching television with a pair of 25-pound dumbbells in his hands, pumping them up and down.

In his collection of equipment, Bruce used two types of speed bags: the old suspended one and the modern type. He had several heavy bags—one weighed as much as 200 pounds. "I like to swing the heavy bag," he explained, "and if I can stop it with a kick I know I can knock a 400-pound man on his ass."

Bruce also had several other pieces of equipment, like a wooden dummy with four hands and two legs, makiwara, hydraulic kicking aparatus, and several punching and kicking canvas bags.

Mischief in the Man

Bruce was mischievous. He enjoyed demonstrating various pieces of his equipment to new acquaintances. But in his eagerness to put everything he had into his displays of speed and power, he often frightened away prospective sparring partners. For instance, he had a banana-shaped canvas train-

Outdoor training was a very important part of Bruce Lee's training. Also training with protective gear was vital to the development of jeet kune do for the advantage of allowing contact with one's opponent, giving a fuller understanding of real combat.

19

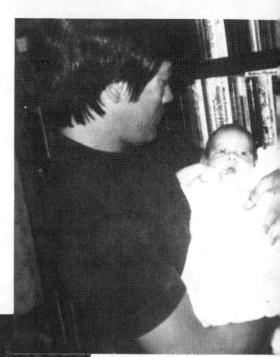

Though physically very powerful, as shown (below) demonstrating his "one-inch" punch against one of Chuck Norris' students at the Long Beach Internationals in 1967, Lee was also given to playfulness, as when sparring with Brandon (below right), and tenderness with new-born daughter Shannon (right).

ing shield which football players use. When filled with air, it was about 12 inches thick and about three feet long. When he met someone for the first time, he quickly coerced the visitor into holding the equipment. Someone would stand about five feet behind the visitor. Bruce would stand about ten feet away, then rush toward the target, applying a hard side kick. The impact from his kick was so powerful it would lift the holder off his feet. The person standing behind him was supposed to catch him, but many times both men would be left sprawling on the ground.

Bruce had three canvas punching bags in his garage. In one bag he had placed beans, in another, sand, and in the third, metal sawdust, which was hard as rock. When an innocent newcomer came around, Bruce would punch one of the soft bags with the sand or beans and let his guest follow suit. Then Bruce would punch the metal sawdust bag with all his strength. When the guest struck the bag and hollered in pain, Bruce would burst out with a hearty laugh.

Bruce demonstrated his one-inch punch at tournaments and social gatherings. He would ask a volunteer to stand upright, holding an inch-thick pad to his chest. Bruce would then place a chair about six feet behind him. With his fist only an inch from the pad, Bruce would send a hardly noticeable punch to his volunteer. The short-distance punch always amazed the volunteer and the witnesses because of its devastating effect. It would propel the person backward, crashing him into the chair, which would topple over because of the impact.

When Bruce performed this technique at the 1967 Long Beach International Karate Championships, his volunteer was Bob Baker of Stockton, California. "I told Bruce not to do this type of demonstration again," Baker recalls. "When he punched me that last time, I had to stay home from work because the pain in my chest was unbearable."

Because Bruce had no interest in sports other than boxing and the martial arts, he had never heard of basketball's Kareem Abdul-Jabbar (Lew Alcindor then) and only became interested in meeting the giant when he learned that he was over seven feet tall. "I'd sure like to spar with him," Bruce once remarked. "I'd like to know how fast he can move and whether I can penetrate his defense." After their initial meeting. Big Lew became Bruce's student for many years. Eventually this relationship led to the making of *Game of Death*, but the Hong Kong movie was only half completed at the time of Bruce's death.

Although Bruce knew many movie stars, producers, and directors, his social life centered mostly around his students and other martial artists. When he became the biggest box-office draw in Asia, he was constantly

At two years of age, Brandon Lee is put through his paces by his father. Here, Bruce challenges the enthusiastic toddler to kick a stick held just within his range. In later years, Brandon would begin his formal training with his father's protege, Dan Inosanto.

bombarded with invitations to accept various awards. "I'd rather spend my time studying or training," he would say. "Awards or trophies are just ornaments. Who needs them?" Some critics assailed Bruce as being swellheaded for not attending these functions. But he sincerely felt that these events were a waste of time. He would rather discuss fighting techniques with other martial artists than "brush shoulders with celebrities."

Another Side of Bruce

Many knew Bruce as a talkative person with hands and feet to back up whatever he claimed. But not many knew that Bruce was also a temperamental individual. When he moved to Culver City from Inglewood, he tried to help his wife by putting a bed together. When he couldn't get it together immediately, he began to cuss and finally drove the bed through the wall. "He sure left a big dent in the wall," laughed Linda.

The summer of 1971 was the turning point in Bruce's life. While going through his regular workouts, he decided to develop his back muscles. Although he knew how to train with weights (he had been using them for years), he made a gross error that moment. He placed an excessive amount of weight on his back shoulders and bent forward. Suddenly he heard a snap, followed by excruciating pain. He knew he had injured his back and immediately dropped the barbell.

While recuperating in bed during the following weeks, Bruce's income completely ceased. He was offered $10,000 to teach his art to a group of

European industrial millionaires for two weeks but had to reject the offer. "This was the first time in my life I was really scared," Bruce confided. "If I hadn't had a family, it wouldn't have been so bad. But having a wife and two children (his daughter, Shannon, had just been born) made me realize that having bread is important."

According to one reliable source, Bruce had only $50 in his bank account after paying off all the medical bills. But he would not ask for, nor accept, money from his friends. When he bought a home in Bel-Air, actor Steve Mc-Queen offered to give him the down payment, but Bruce declined the help. Later, when McQueen offered to pay for his Porsche, Bruce again refused.

Those few weeks bound to his bed were unbearable for Bruce. He could hardly keep still. "I never wanted a job in an office or any job that I had to work eight hours a day at—day in and day out," he used to say. "I don't think I could have stood it." But the weeks in which he had to remain in bed —or, at least, idle—gave him time to think. He finally realized he couldn't make a living just teaching jeet kune do to Hollywood celebrities.

"I was determined then to be an actor," Bruce said. "Not just an actor, but a star." He then began to outline a story for a script: *The Silent Flute*. At the same time, he compiled a rough for a book called *The Tao of Jeet Kune Do*. His third effort was a book eventually entitled *Wing Chun Kung Fu*,

With his Way of the Dragon *co-star Chuck Norris, Bruce had many screen fights, but they were the best of friends off screen. The incredible fight between Lee and Norris which takes place at the climax of the story, has since become a classic scene in the genre of martial arts films.*

which was completed and published by Ohara Publications, Inc., Bruce didn't want his name to appear as author of the book because he felt that wing chun was not his style anymore. So he decided to use a pseudonym. But just before the book went into publication, he gave it to his close friend James Lee, who was suffering from a serious illness.

The Silent Flute

Meanwhile, Bruce met with Academy Award-winning writer Stirling Silliphant and actor James Coburn to work out details on *The Silent Flute*. The three men formed a joint venture and presented the project to Warner Bros. Warner's liked it but didn't want to put a heavy production budget into it. So they decided to shoot it in India, but the project failed when one of the men became disenchanted with the location. Bruce was very disappointed by this turn of events. He had been counting heavily on this film to open the door to stardom.

Even before he became a box-office draw, Bruce had always had a rapport with youngsters. During his co-starring role in *The Green Hornet*, he was bombarded with invitations to attend parades or other events where children usually congregate. He loved to kid around with them and sign

Although Lee was very active in his Way of the Dragon *which he not only directed but also starred in (right), he still found time to greet old friends, such as James Coburn (above) when they arrived at Hong Kong's Kai Tak Airport. Coburn was also one of Lee's jeet kune do students.*

24

Lee sank himself into his Way of the Dragon *role 24 hours a day and he supervised the moving of locations from Hong Kong to Rome where he relied on the help of his two old friends, Chuck Norris and Bob Wall. In later years, Wall would reflect, "It was always exciting to work with Bruce because he was always teaching you something."*

autographs. One of his favorite tricks was to place a dime in the hand of an unsuspecting boy or girl. "You can keep the dime if you are faster than me," he would encourage the youngster. "But before I take it away from you, I want you to have some practice." He would place a dime in the child's outstretched hand and would then tell him to close his hand before he could take it. The first couple of times, he would take the dime away and say, "You are too slow. Let's try it one more time." On the third attempt, the child would gleefully exclaim, "I've got it! I've got it!" only to find, upon opening his fist, that the dime had been replaced with a penny. Bruce's movement had been so swift that the youngster hadn't even noticed the switch.

The five-foot, seven-inch superstar was soft-hearted in many ways. When an admirer, a virtual stranger, asked to stay at his home, Bruce could not refuse. One such visitor stayed with him for over a week, but Bruce didn't have the heart to tell the visitor to pack up and go.

Bruce was a compassionate person. In October, 1972, when he returned to the United States to negotiate a contract with Sequoia Pictures to do *Enter the Dragon,* he was upset by the condition of his best friend, James Lee, of Oakland, California. James (no relation to Bruce) had cancer and Bruce knew that his friend had only a few months left to live.

"I've invited Jimmy to Hong Kong for the premier of *Way of the Dragon,*" Bruce mentioned. "I sure wish the doctor would let him come. I want him to at least see Hong Kong before he goes. It sure will be hard if he passes away in Hong Kong, but it'll be much harder to bid farewell to a close pal you know you'll never see again. Boy, I'm emotional that way and I don't know how to take it."

James Lee never got to Hong Kong. On December 30, 1972, Bruce called directly from Hong Kong to inform a friend in Los Angeles that James had

Bruce and student James Lee clown around at a photo session for the book Wing Chun Kung Fu *(far right). At that time some notable Lee roles included parts in* The Green Hornet *with Van Williams (below right),* Marlowe *with James Garner (below), and later, starring in* Way of the Dragon *(left) and* Enter the Dragon *(right).*

died. Bruce was so emotionally distraught, he could hardly speak. The relationship between the two men had been a very close one for many years. When James' wife had been stricken with cancer in the 60s, Bruce and Linda remained with their friend until he had overcome his grief.

A Philosophical Way of Life

Although Bruce attended Catholic schools during his childhood, he was not religious. He could recite the Bible by heart but never mentioned the Almighty. It is possible that he got so much religion while he was young, he shut himself off from it. "The only time I heard him mention prayer," said an acquaintance, "is when Steve McQueen drove down Mulholland Drive. 'Steve drove like he was in an auto race,' Bruce told me, 'and I was holding my seat and praying for my life. I kept thinking, what if he hits a stone? There's no tomorrow."

Bruce had only a year left at the University of Washington, where he ma-

jored in philosophy, when he left for Oakland. He wasn't a good student—
"barely made passing grades." But he was erudite in Oriental philosophy
(Taoism, Zen, etc.) and seemed to have been influenced more by Oriental
philosophy than Christianity.

The success that Bruce achieved in so short a time would have bewildered
most young actors, but not Bruce. In 1970, he had a reading from a Las
Vegas astrologer. "She predicted that 1971 will be my year," he said. "But
I've already had this feeling that my time for success is here. I can just about
taste it." Bruce spoke dogmatically—almost to the point of obsession—as
though nothing would stop him until he reached the top.

Then when the breaks came, they came from all over. Paramount produced a TV series called *Longstreet,* with James Franciscus in the starring
role. Stirling Silliphant, who did the screenplay, wrote one of the scripts
specifically with Bruce in mind. "Way of the Fist" was scheduled to be aired
on the fourth week of the new series, but because of Bruce's fine perfor-

Bruce's dramatic talents led him from the TV show Longstreet *with James Franciscus (below) to the starring role in* Enter the Dragon *(left).*

mance, the producer opened the series with the segment. The reviews from the trade papers and others like the *Los Angeles Times* and *New York Times* were gratifying. "First time in my life that I had any kind of review for my acting," Bruce said. "I'm glad they were favorable."

Then in July of 1971, Bruce left California for Bangkok, Thailand, to shoot *The Big Boss*. For the first time, Bruce had a starring role in a movie. He was given some voice by producer Raymond Chow, of Golden Harvest, Ltd., in Hong Kong, and he took advantage of the experience he had gained in Hollywood, especially in choreographing the fight scenes.

"Most Chinese movies followed the Japanese, and there were too many weapons—especially swords," Bruce explained. "So we used a minimum of weapons and made it into a better film."

The Big Boss broke all records in Hong Kong. It grossed $3.2 million (Hong Kong), surpassing *Sound of Music*, which had held the record for a number of years at $2.8 million (H.K.) *The Big Boss* also broke records in other countries, including the Philippines, Singapore, Malaysia, and other parts of Asia.

No Long-Term Contracts

While Bruce was shooting his first starring role in a motion picture, Paramount was desperately looking for him after the fall opener of *Longstreet*.

"They couldn't get in touch with me because I was really in the sticks. We were so far out that we couldn't even get meat. I had only vegetables and rice, and I lost ten pounds."

Paramount wanted Bruce to be a regular on *Longstreet,* but he only appeared in three more segments. He didn't have the time now to alter any of the scripts to fit his acting, as he had done in the first episode, so he felt his subsequent appearances were not as dynamic as his role in the opener. "I was getting offers from MGM and Warner Bros.," Bruce admitted, "and didn't want to be tied to a long contract." Besides, Bruce was already the biggest box-office draw in the Far East, and his enthusiasm for the additional TV segments had waned with the prospects for movies.

When his second movie, *Fists of Fury,* hit the Hong Kong theaters, it established another record, outgrossing *The Big Boss* by $1.3 million. It recorded big gains in other countries, too. In the Philippines, *Fists of Fury* ran for over six months with full capacity, and the government finally had to limit the amount of foreign film imports to protect their domestic producers.

In Singapore, scalpers were getting $45 for a $2.00 ticket. On opening night, hundreds of movie patrons rushed to the theater, causing such a traffic jam that they had to postpone showing the movie for a week until the

Armed with a pair of kali sticks in a scene from Enter the Dragon, *Bruce gets set to take on all comers in a heroic attempt to free innocent prisoners.*

authorities could find a way to resolve the problem. It was the first movie jam in Singapore's history.

Offers came from other movie producers who couldn't compete against Bruce's films. Run Run Shaw, of Hong Kong, made a spectacular and unusual offer—$2 million for one film—which was headlined in one of the local newspapers.

"I had a heck of a problem after my movies became a smash," said Lee. "Strangers would stop at my door and just hand me checks for thousands of dollars. When I would ask them what the money was for, they'd reply, 'Don't worry about it; it's just a gift to you.' "

Although Bruce never accepted such gifts, the number of offers began to affect him. "It was very bewildering. I didn't know whom to trust and I even grew suspicious of my old pals. I was in a period when I didn't know who was trying to take advantage of me."

After his second movie, Bruce formed his own production company—Concorde—with Raymond Chow as his partner. Their first joint effort, *Way of the Dragon*, was particularly important to Lee because he not only wrote the script, but starred in, directed, and produced the movie. "I worked almost around the clock for days and lost several more pounds," Bruce said. "I did it because it was fun. It was something I had always had an in-

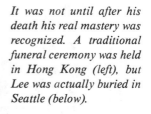

It was not until after his death his real mastery was recognized. A traditional funeral ceremony was held in Hong Kong (left), but Lee was actually buried in Seattle (below).

terest in. I got hold of a dozen books on film production and direction and really dug into them.''

When the superstar predicted in the trades and dailies that his third movie would surpass a $5-million take in Hong Kong, the movie critics really put Bruce down. "How could a movie outgross *Sound of Music* by almost two times?" they scoffed. But the upstart movie hero made the critics eat their words. The latest movie re-established a new record: $5.4 million.

Lee's *Way of the Dragon* was the first Hong Kong movie ever to go to Europe for location shooting. "The movie was a little more costly from a Hong Kong standard, but we got our returns right away," Bruce was quick to point out. "Before it even opened, we had already sold the distribution rights to Taiwan for the whole production cost."

Enter the Dragon

Although Bruce felt that the first three movies he had participated in were not intended for the American public, *Enter the Dragon* was definitely for the American, European, and Oriental viewers. The movie became a hit around the world. Surpassed only by *My Fair Lady*, it was the second biggest money-maker for Warner Bros. in their foreign distribution history, grossing over $14 million (U.S.). In the United States and Canada alone, it grossed $6.5 million.

Just before his death, Bruce was offered $2 million (U.S.) to do two movies in Hungary. Warner Bros. also wanted him to do five features. "Ashley (Ted Ashley, president of Warner Bros.) told me they would not pay a million dollars for my services but they could make other lucrative arrangements," Bruce confided.

On July 20, 1973, the young superstar died a controversial death. The coroner's report was inconclusive, and five medical authorities came up with five different reasons for Bruce Lee's untimely death. They agreed that it was caused by a cerebral edema (a congestion or buildup of fluid in the brain), but they could not agree on what had caused the edema. The most reasonable explanation in the coroner's report seems to be that Bruce developed an allergy to the medication he was taking for his injured back.

It is unfortunate that Bruce was not able to witness the full impact of his accomplishments. His dream of being the biggest Oriental star in the world was almost in his grasp—just a few more months and he would have done it.

But death was a subject Bruce had openly discussed with his most intimate friends. "If I should die tomorrow," he used to reiterate, "I will have no regrets. I did what I wanted to do. You can't expect much more from life."

PART 2

Chapter 2

Was "The Green Hornet's" Version of Kung Fu Genuine?

by Maxwell Pollard

During the period he performed in *The Green Hornet* TV show as Kato and astonished the American public (especially its youth) with their first look at kung fu, Bruce Lee said there was too much hocus-pocus about the martial arts.

Bruce, (who was Cantonese and preferred to pronounce his art as "gung fu" instead of "kung fu") contended that some martial arts instructors couldn't stand the gaff if they became involved in a streetfight.

All of their knowledge about forms and stances wouldn't do them any good. He charged that some teachers favored forms, the fancier and more complex, the better, and seemed to be obsessed with super-mental power like Captain Marvel or Superman.

Bruce admitted that he himself contributed primarily to the theatrical aspects of this ancient Chinese art that dates back several thousands years, but he did it for the sake of dramatic effect. For instance, in a close-quarter encounter with a villain or a group of villains, the script may have called for Kato to uncork some devastating kicks to the head.

Any hood with even a smidgeon of knowledge of self-defense would immediately knock you off balance if you tried to use your legs in that fashion when you're trading blows up close, Lee explained. The real kung fu would call for a much wiser line of attack.

As far as the TV show was concerned, it was flashy and full of showmanship, but, as Bruce explained in his clipped British accent: "Some of the techniques used are not what I practice in kung fu. For instance, I never

Virtually unknown at that time, kung fu received public exposure when Bruce used it to combat villains in The Green Hornet. *At first, only an exotic element, it soon became one of the show's primary attractions.*

believe in jumping and kicking. My kicks in actual kung fu are not high but low, to the shin and the groin.''

Even if the director insisted on it, Bruce Lee would not permit kung fu to be put in a bad light on TV just for the sake of heightening the action. He refused to go along with any suggestions for long, drawn out, Western styles of brawling, despite calls for this type of fighting in the script.

The Green Hornet went to a limit of 30 weeks and could have gone longer but for the sad fact that it lacked realism and played it straight instead of satirically. Folks just refused to believe the masked characters were real.

In the story, Bruce Lee co-starred with Van Williams who played Britt Reid. As Kato, Bruce played the faithful friend and companion to Reid as the crusading, crime-busting newspaperman from the *Daily Sentinel.* The latter adopted the guise of the Green Hornet in his fight against crime and corruption, with Kato serving as bodyguard.

Behind their black masks, they set out with a grim determination as a two-man vigilante committee to uphold law and decency in the community and they did a thoroughly efficient job of exterminating the troublemakers. And they always did it in short order.

Bruce was more than a Hollywood actor. He was a man who took kung fu seriously. A vibrant personality with piercing black eyes and a rather handsome face full of animation, unlike the inscrutable poker-faced expressions Westerners usually associate with the Oriental, Lee looked like the actor that he was. Yet, he actually lived the role of the clean-living martial arts hero that he played on TV.

Lee neither smoked nor drank, and he strove to keep physically fit at all times. Even before breakfast, he started the day with a mile-and-a-half run with his Great Dane dog Bobo, two-finger push-ups, and additional workouts in the afternoon. On weekends, he headed for Chinatown for more sparring. The five-foot eight-inch, 145-pound advocate of kung fu was as springy as a cat, and his hands were quicker than the eye.

Although in *The Green Hornet* he disposed of the bad guys in short order, there were suspenseful moments during the 30-week run of the TV series when Kato had to employ every trick in the bag to rescue the Green Hornet from the mob's clutches.

Even though Kato's techniques were not always genuine because even Bruce had to bend a little to meet the dictates of the script, this was no reason to suspect his expertise. Actually, Bruce had been a student of this mixture of Western fencing and boxing since he was 13 years old (he was only 26 at the time of the series).

Bruce taught his wife Linda techniques of kung fu so that she would be able to defend herself if anyone ever dared to attack her, and said he also intended to give Brandon, (Shannon was born later), a martial arts education as he grew up.

However, Bruce Lee stressed that when it comes to women, he had no illusions about their ability to defend themselves against a brute, even a big one.

"I advise any female learning kung fu that if they are ever attacked, to hit 'em in the groin, poke 'em in the eyeballs, kick 'em on the shins, or the knee . . . and run like hell," he said.

Bruce was probably the highest paid martial arts instructor in the business. Teaching was what he did when he was not performing before the cameras. He charged $50 an hour when he went to the home of a student and

Posing for a publicity photo (above left) with co-star Van Williams and George Trendle, the creator of The Green Hornet. *Bruce's role on the show was the beginning of a new phase in his career. At the same time, Linda kept up with her own self-defense training, here practicing an escape technique with Ted Wong (above right). Even Brandon (left) got into the spirit with his front kicks.*

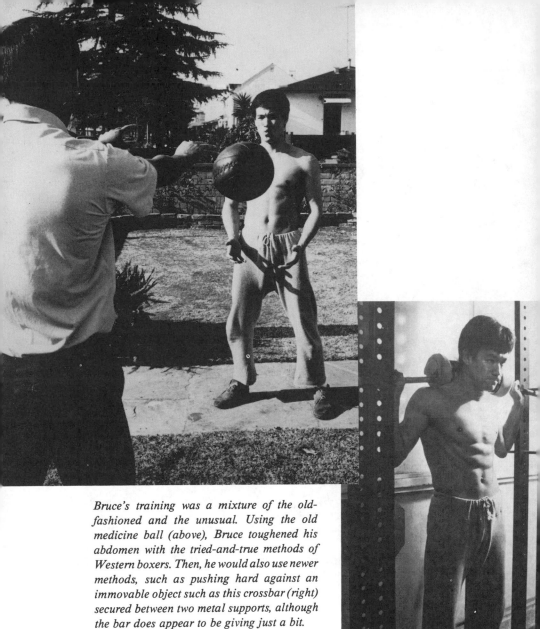

Bruce's training was a mixture of the old-fashioned and the unusual. Using the old medicine ball (above), Bruce toughened his abdomen with the tried-and-true methods of Western boxers. Then, he would also use newer methods, such as pushing hard against an immovable object such as this crossbar (right) secured between two metal supports, although the bar does appear to be giving just a bit.

$27.50 an hour when the student came to his club—sometimes more. This included actors, businessmen, and high-ranking karate instructors.

"If I find a black belt who likes to spar, I charge nothing because I really enjoy the company," he said.

Bruce Lee operated three clubs or *kwoons* as they were called in Chinese. They were located in Seattle, Oakland, and Los Angeles. In Seattle, the

Finger-jabbing techniques are a very important part of Bruce's original style, wing chun. These techniques, he found, were practical and effective, and so he kept training in them even after his style had changed. Intended for striking precise targets such as nerve centers, they required strong fingers. Bruce regularly practiced his finger jabs against specially designed targets.

kwoon was directed by Tak Kimura; in Oakland, it was simply called "The James Lee"; in Los Angeles, the club was located in Chinatown and directed by Danny Inosanto. They were all non-commercial and there are no signs anywhere on the outside to identify the establishments.

Bruce Lee was not given to exploiting his name at these kwoons. There was a time when he thought seriously of establishing a chain of schools under his name across the country, but he didn't think it was the right thing to do because as he said, "I don't think money is everything."

Interest in kung fu increased steadily since *The Green Hornet* went on the air. Because the masked characters played it straight instead of gagging it up in satire, the series didn't turn out to be another eternal *Bonanza*. Nevertheless, it helped stir interest in the ancient Chinese art.

Bruce Lee appearances were in demand in many parts of the country. He put on demonstrations at fairs, public parks, and at club meetings, and was paid anywhere from $2,000 to $3,000 for a single appearance.

While *The Green Hornet* didn't capture any Emmys, there was a widespread demand for reruns, and it was syndicated not only in this country but on TV stations in Japan, Thailand, Argentina, Puerto Rico, and Canada.

"I never know where it's showing until the fan letters start coming in," he related.

Bruce made a guest appearance in *Ironside*, starring Raymond Burr, and more movie contracts appeared on the horizon as producers became aware of this talented young Chinese athlete/actor.

Wherever he went, fans were happy just to touch him, even if they didn't

Bruce was perfect as Kato. Sleek as a cat, and blessed with great speed, he could do everything in real life that Kato was called on to do on the screen.

Hard work was the reality behind the illusion. Bruce's prowess as a martial artist propelled him to stardom, but years of dedicated training laid the groundwork. Knowing this, Bruce never stopped training.

get his autograph. They wanted to meet "Kato" and they wanted to know how he was able to knock off those bad guys so quickly.

"This sometimes becomes a terrifying experience," said Bruce. "After my personal appearance in Madison Square Garden at the karate tournament, I started to make an exit through a side door escorted by three karatemen. I was practically mobbed outside and I had to leave through another side door." Earlier, in a personal appearance in Fresno, he was scratched, kicked, and gouged by riotous fans who just wanted a word with him. The kids were out in full force.

With all his knowledge of kung fu, he said afterward, "I couldn't protect myself."

About 60 percent of the fans were boys, and it was surprising the number of girls who adored this TV idol.

"People ask me as an actor, 'how good are you really in kung fu?' I always kid them about that. If I tell them I'm good, they'll probably say I'm boasting, but if I tell them I'm no good, you know I'm lying. And so, I tell them 'believe half of what you see and nothing that you hear—and remember, 700 million Chinese can't be Wong.' "

Chapter 3

In Kato's Kung Fu, Action Was Instant

by Maxwell Pollard

On assignments for BLACK BELT magazine, this reporter had several long talks with the dynamic, effervescent Bruce Lee about his work and his art.

As Kato in *The Green Hornet*, Bruce Lee was a stickler for realism. Even after the series ended, if a TV producer asked him to play a role, Bruce wanted to know before he signed up whether the part was reasonably realistic.

Lee did let the bars down a wee bit when he accepted the role of body-guard and faithful companion to the Green Hornet by hoking up his kung fu tactics to provide more exciting action. But, the San Francisco-born, Hong Kong-raised, actor learned some valuable lessons from his initial experience in the world of make-believe.

"Some time ago," Bruce once related, "I was offered a number-one spot in a proposed one-hour series titled *Number-One Son* (Son of Charlie Chan) and it was going to be like a Chinese James Bond-type of thing. I wanted to make sure before I signed that there wouldn't be any 'ah-so's' and 'chop-chops' in the dialogue and that I would not be required to go bouncing around with a pigtail."

The deal never did materialize but Bruce had the inner satisfaction of knowing that he wasn't about to submit to movie stereotypes and that he would never do anything that might degrade the Oriental race from which he sprang.

And when it came to Chinese kung fu, Bruce also insisted on realism and plausibility. There were many different schools of kung fu in Hong Kong, according to Bruce, and like in the United States, it was difficult to find worthwhile instruction.

"Too much horsing around with unrealistic stances and classic forms

Kato's mask could not hide Bruce's individuality. The discipline of the martial arts gave Bruce the determination to remain true to himself. From the very start, Bruce's characters were graced with his own fierce self-pride.

and rituals," said Bruce. "It's just too artificial and mechanical and doesn't really prepare a student for actual combat. A guy could get clobbered while getting into his classical mess. Classical methods like these, which I consider a form of paralysis, only solidify and condition what was once fluid. Their practitioners are merely blindly rehearsing systematic routines and stunts that will lead to nowhere."

Bruce characterized this type of teaching as nothing more than "organized despair."

Basically, his technique was to proceed instantly and unceremoniously to knock his adversary flat on his wallet before he could even remember why he picked on him in the first place.

Lightning movements played an important part in Bruce's techniques. To perfect his speed, Bruce developed an extraordinarily quick eye and uncanny fast hands.

As must be obvious by now, the buoyant young expert in the Chinese art of kung fu took a dim view of the classical versions of this ancient martial art.

"To me, a lot of this fancy stuff is not functional," he said. And, he tried to prove it through the three kung fu kwoons he operated in Seattle,

Bruce never forgot his wing chun techniques. The traditional wing chun training dummy with its three arms and one leg was one of the most important pieces of equipment in Bruce's gym. Here, he shows how block and counterstrike constitute a single action.

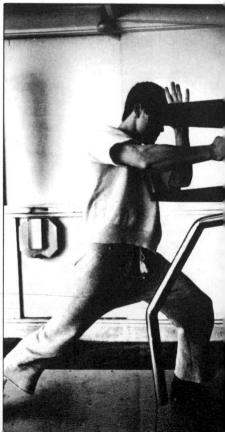

Oakland, and in Los Angeles' Chinatown. All featured *jeet kune do* (Chinese boxing). Bruce called his establishments the Jun Fan Kung Fu Institute (Bruce's Chinese name was Jun Fan). Because they were "exclusive" establishments, none bore any commercial signs on the outside to identify it. However, as Bruce pointed out, "The 'in groups' know where they are."

He did not teach publicly. His students were carefully chosen. They were mostly instructors of different styles and took instruction at these kwoons once a week. Occasionally, when he felt up to it, Bruce taught private lessons, and some of these private students flew in all the way from the East Coast.

"These private lessons are usually not interesting," Bruce related, "it is more enjoyable to teach those who have gone through conventional training. They understand and appreciate what I have to offer.

A Memorial

To get a closer look at Bruce Lee's techniques, I once visited his kwoon in Los Angeles' Chinatown. I immediately got the message as I stepped through the front door. Near the entrance, my eyes fell on a miniature tombstone embellished with a bouquet of flowers. Inscribed on the tombstone were the cryptic words: *In memory of a once fluid man, crammed and distorted by the classical mess.*

"That expresses my feelings perfectly," Bruce explained as he stripped down to his undershirt and trousers and went into a two-hour practice session with Daniel Lee, a friend and stalwart adherent of Bruce's jeet kune do.

Bruce moved about the kwoon like a panther, counterattacking moving in, punching with great power from the hips. Occasionally, shin kicks, finger jabs, powerful body punches to the solar-plexus, use of elbows and knees. I noted that Bruce's body was constantly relaxed.

The movements were like those of a polished, highly-refined prizefighter delivering his blows with subtle economy. There seemed to be a mixture of Western fencing and the wing chun style wrapped up in Bruce Lee's techniques of Chinese kung fu. Yet, his jeet kune do was unlike any existing style.

During his workout with Daniel Lee, Bruce, showing hardly a sign of hard breathing, would pause to explain to me what jeet kune do was all about.

Bruce described it himself this way: "The extraordinary part of it lies in its simplicity. Every movement in jeet kune do is being so of itself. There is nothing articifical about it. I always believe that the easy way is the right way. Jeet kune do is simply the direct expression of one's feelings with the

Bruce shows student Dan Lee (above) the advantages of taking control of the center. Another view of the same exchange (right) reveals how Dan's front punch is deflected away by Bruce's forearm coming through the center of Dan's defense. Bruce effectively delivers a strike at the same time that he protects himself from Dan's attempt—an example of directness.

minimum of movements and energy. The closer to the true way of kung fu, the less wastage of expression there is.

"There is no mystery about my style. My movements are *simple, direct* and *non-classical*. Before I discuss jeet kune do, I would like to stress the fact that though my present style is more totally alive and efficient, I owe my achievement to my previous training in the wing chun style, a great style. It was taught to me by Yip Man, leader of the wing chun clan in Hong Kong where I was reared.

"Jeet kune do is the only non-classical style of Chinese kung fu in existence today. It is simple in its execution, although not so simple to explain. *Jeet* means 'to stop, to stalk, to intercept' while *kune* means 'fist' or 'style' and *do* means 'the way' or the 'ultimate reality.'

"In other words, 'The Way of the Stopping Fist.' The main characteristic of this style is the absence of the usual classical passive blocking. Blocking is the least efficient. Jeet kune do is offensive, it's alive and it's free."

Bruce also pointed out, and with great emphasis, that there were no classical forms or sets in the system because they tended to be rhythmic. He liked broken rhythm and said, "Classical forms are futile attempts to arrest and fix the ever-changing movements in combat and to dissect and analyze them like a corpse."

What he was dealing with, explained Bruce, was "the actual reality of combat," with none of the abstractions that set up a simulated exchange resembling anything from acrobatics to modern dancing.

"When in actual combat," Bruce stressed, "you're not fighting a corpse. Your opponent is a living, moving object who is not in a fixed position, but fluid and alive. Deal with him realistically, not as though you're fighting a robot."

Unlike other styles that practice in rhythm, which Bruce called "two-man cooperation," jeet kune do uses broken rhythm in both training and sparring.

As I watched Bruce through his workouts, I became intrigued by his continual emphasis on non-classicism, directness and his insistence on simplicity.

"Can you explain just what you mean when you say 'being non-classical?' " I asked.

"Traditionally, classical forms and efficiency are both equally important," Bruce declared. "I'm not saying form is not important, economy of form that is, but to me, efficiency is anything that scores.

"To illustrate my point, let me tell you a story: Two Orientals were watching the Olympic Games in Rome. One of the chief attractions was Bob Hayes, the sprinter, in the 100-yard run. As the gun went off to set the race in motion, the spectators leaned forward in their seats, tense with excitement. With the runners nearing their goal, Hayes forged ahead and flashed across the line, the winner with a new world's record of 9.1 seconds. As the

Bruce often bested his friend and student Dan Lee in "sticky hands" while blindfolded (below). This exercise was for improving his feeling for parrying and countering. To improve his speed, he used special training equipment (right).

crowd cheered, one of the Orientals elbowed the other in the ribs and whispered, 'Did you see that? His heel was up.' "

"I don't have to be hit over the head—I get the point," I said. "What then do you mean when you say, 'directness?' "

I had hardly gotten the words out of my mouth when Bruce's wallet came flying at me. Automatically, I reached up and grabbed it in midair.

Comes Naturally

When I regained my composure, Bruce said, "That's directness. You did what comes naturally. You didn't waste time. You just reached up and caught the wallet—and you didn't squat, grunt, or go into a horse stance or embark on some such classical move before reaching out for the wallet. You wouldn't have caught it if you had."

Bruce paused a moment then continued, "In other words, when someone grabs you, punch him! Don't indulge in any unnecessary, sophisticated moves! You'll get clobbered if you do and in a streetfight, you'll have your shirt ripped off of you."

"All right, Bruce," I said, warming to the subject, "now I understand what you mean when you speak of directness. Now, let's elaborate a little on the last of the three essentials of jeet kune do—simplicity."

"The best illustration is something I borrowed from *Chan* (Zen)," Bruce began. "Before I studied the art, a punch to me was just a punch, a kick just a kick. After I learned the art, a punch is no longer a punch, a kick no longer a kick. Now that I've understood the art, a punch is just like a punch, a kick just like a kick.

"The height of cultivation is really nothing special. It is merely simplicity, the ability to express the utmost with the minimum. It is the half-way cultivation that leads to ornamentation."

Bruce laid emphasis on the fact that adherents of jeet kune do do not indulge themselves with fancy embellishment.

"It is basically a sophisticated fighting style stripped to its essentials," Bruce explained. "The disciples are very proud to be accepted in this exclusive style."

The actor/kung fu expert stressed over and over again that he didn't believe in loading up his techniques with all sorts of "superficialities," as he called them. He liked to compare his art to the work of a sculptor.

"In building a statue," Bruce said, "a sculptor doesn't keep adding clay to his subject. Actually, he begins chiseling away at the unessentials until the truth of his creation is revealed without obstructions.

"Thus, contrary to other styles, being wise in jeet kune do doesn't mean

With the uncomplicated side kick, Bruce could generate more sheer power than any other type of kick. He often sent his partners who held the kicking bag flying in the opposite direction. The side kick thrusts all of the body's energy in a single direction. Expressing this directness was the kind of release of personal power Bruce found liberating.

adding more. It means to minimize. In other words, to hack away at the unessentials. It is not a 'daily increase' but a 'daily decrease.' The way of jeet kune do is a shedding process.

"In short, jeet kune do is satisfied with one's bare hands without the fancy decoration of colorful gloves which hinder the natural function of the hand."

Bruce Lee studied philosophy at Washington University and he was an avid student of Zen, Taoism, and Christianity. And when the time was appropriate he would philosophize.

"Art," he observed, "is really the expression of the self. The more complicated and restricted the method, the less the opportunity for the expression of one's original sense of freedom.

"Though they play an important role in the early stage, the techniques should not be too mechanical, complex or restrictive. If we blindly cling to them, we will eventually become bound by their limitations.

"Remember, you are *expressing* the techniques and not *doing* the techniques. If somebody attacks you, your response is not Technique No. 1, Stance No. 2, Section 4, Paragraph 5. Instead, you simply move in like sound and echo, without any deliberation.

"It is as though, when I call you, you answer me, or when I throw something at you, you catch it. It's as simple as that, no fuss, no muss."

To keep on top of his craft, Bruce Lee exercised religiously and did it every day. A mile-and-a-half run through a field near his Southern California home, followed by supplementary exercises, plus an hour-and-a-half of daily workouts in jeet kune do.

"Prevention is better than cure," Bruce said. "I'm still young (he was 26 years old at the time), but I'd like to maintain my level as much as possible when I pass the 40 mark.''

Only in the Oriental martial arts, said Bruce, are there champions at the age of 99. If a man spends 20 years training, by the time he finishes, he's too old to do anything unless the training began at a very early age.

''You do not get better as you grow older—you only get wiser,'' Bruce observed with traditional Oriental wisdom.

I asked Bruce about the rumors that he wore a gray sash as a kung fu teacher. ''I'm sorry, but I myself know nothing of it,'' he answered.

''But there are rankings in kung fu, aren't there?'' I persisted.

''Not in traditional kung fu,'' he replied. ''However, we do have a

Bruce liked the old-fashioned speed bag to improve correct punching and footwork. It also taught him timing since the bag recoiled as fast as it was punched.

48

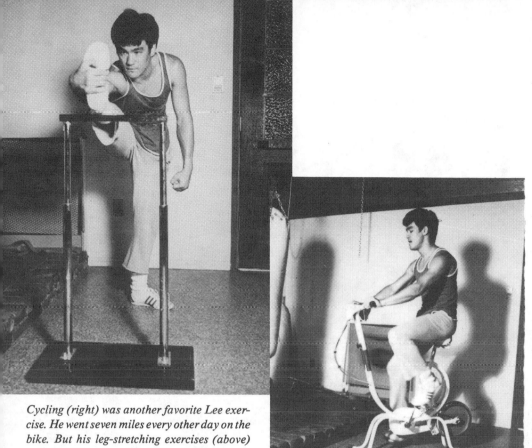

Cycling (right) was another favorite Lee exercise. He went seven miles every other day on the bike. But his leg-stretching exercises (above) were "it." They gave him the flexibility to move with the kind of freedom he liked.

unique ranking system of no ranking. The first rank is a blank circle which signifies original freedom. The second rank is green and white in the form of the *yin yang* symbol with two curved arrows around it. The third is purple and white, the fourth is gray and white, the fifth is red and white, the sixth is gold and white, the seventh is red and gold, which is our school's emblem, and the eighth is the highest, which is a blank circle, the return to the beginning stage."

Mess Cleaners

Bruce paused and a twinkle came into his coal-black eyes.

"In other words," he added, "all the previous rank certificates are useful for cleaning up messes."

A visitor to Bruce Lee's home became aware immediately that the occupant was pre-occupied with body conditioning and physical culture. Gymnasium equipment greeted the observant eye. It was everywhere, some chrome-plated, some fashioned from special teak wood. There were stuffed

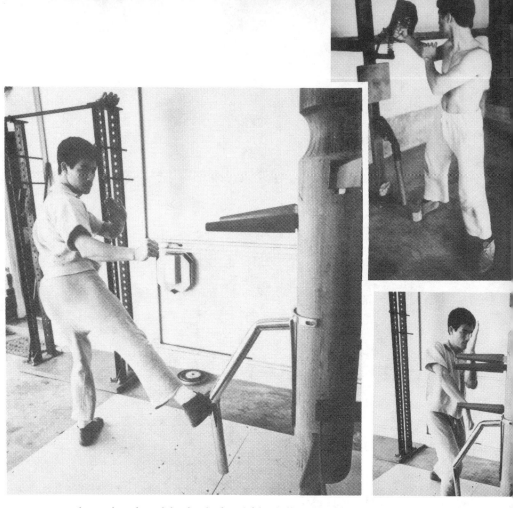

dummies that felt the lash of his daily punching exercises. Most of the facilities were made to order for Bruce and his jeet kune do training. Most of them were originals, not to be found anywhere else.

There were ingenious, yet functional. For instance, a chrome-plated dummy head that gave like a human head when it was on the receiving end of Bruce's lightning fingerjabs to the eyes or throat.

On a weekend, Bruce took himself down to his kwoon to spar with his assistant and a few of his followers.

But he kept a clear perspective on what he was doing.

"No amount of idealistic land swimming will prepare you for the water," he observed. "The best exercise for swimming is swimming. The best exercise for jeet kune do is actual sparring."

Bruce and those who worked out with him wore full protective equipment from head to shin, to avoid injury. He was constantly on the lookout

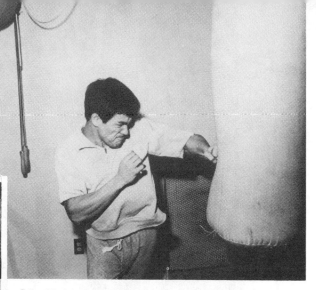

Like his jeet june do, Lee's training combined the traditional and the exotic, Eastern and Western. His only concern was deriving the maximum benefits from the whole available spectrum. The heavy bag (above) helped him develop power. To toughen his hands and strengthen his fingers for thrusting, he used fine gravel (left). For hand techniques (opposite page, bottom) and foot techniques (opposite page, far left) he relied on the wing chun dummy. And for strikes to the head, a special dummy was used (opposite page, top) which employed springs to re-create the realistic reactions that would occur if an actual blow landed to the opponent's head.

for newer equipment and was already in the process of acquiring protective equipment items made of fiberglass.

For many years, kung fu, as a martial art, was played "close to the vest" by its Chinese practitioners who refused to teach it to anyone, except to Chinese. However, the art came out from behind its bamboo curtain to penetrate the outside world. And Bruce Lee, as the explosive Kato of *The Green Hornet* gave it a big boost by popularizing it among all races. As a result, interest in kung fu began to grow in widening circles.

But, Bruce hoped that students would shy away from the quacks and choose wisely before they undertook to learn the art. At that time, Bruce was in the process of writing a book to clear up some of the mysteries involved in kung fu. He had started it in 1963. It was published posthumously in 1975. Its title: *The Tao of Jeet Kune Do.*

"It is indeed difficult," he observed, "to convey simplicity."

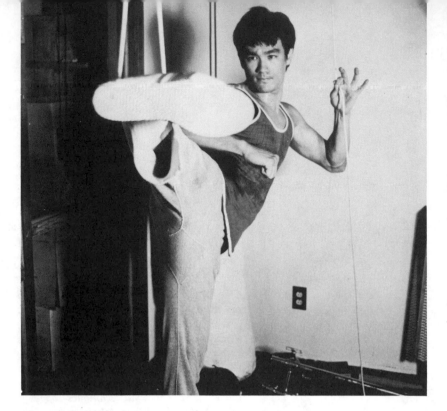

Chapter 4

Bruce Lee's Training Methods

by Mitch Stom

"The only way to teach anyone proper self-defense is to approach each individual personally," said Bruce Lee. "Each one of us is different, and each one of us should be taught the correct form. By correct form I mean the most useful techniques the person is inclined toward. Find his ability and then develop these techniques."

Bruce didn't think it was important if a side kick was performed with the heel higher than the toes, as long as the fundamental principle was not violated. "In most classical martial arts," Bruce contended, "training is a mere imitative repetition—a product—and individuality is lost."

In jeet kune do, Bruce emphasized physical conditioning as a must for all martial artists. "If you are not physically fit," he said, "you have no business doing any hard sparring. To me, the best exercise for this is running. Running is so important that you should keep it up during your lifetime. What time of the day you run is not important as long as you run. In the beginning, you should jog easily, then gradually increase the distance and tempo, and finally include sprinting to develop your wind."

From Monday through Saturday, Bruce ran 15 to 45 minutes (two to six miles) without pausing. At times, he added jeet kune do footwork between the running.

Bruce believed that each individual should include a supplemental training schedule; that is, he should not just rely on training in the gym or school but should have his own training schedule—utilizing different equipment—between the gym training sessions.

Bruce relied on the supplemental training and followed it faithfully to keep in top physical condition. His training emphasized speed, agility, power, flexibility, endurance, timing, and coordination. He also believed in proper nutrition and sufficient rest.

"Just because you get very good at this supplemental training," Bruce warned, "it should not go to your head that you're an expert. Remember,

Bruce Lee was a subscriber to the theory that running was the "king of all exercises." Here he romps with Bobo, his great dane who was a frequent companion on Bruce's daily run around the neighborhood.

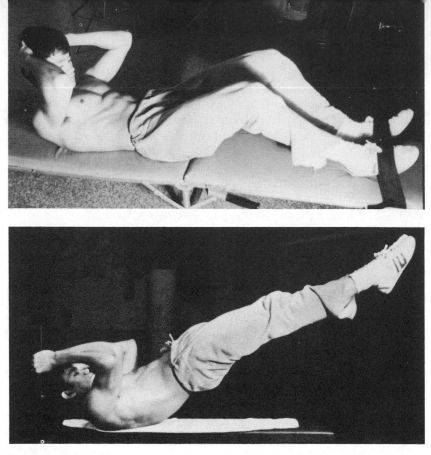

Bruce Lee believed leg raises were a valuable exercise to develop the lower stomach muscles (above). He said to perform that feat, a man needed years of training. His sit-ups (top) were a must for all martial artists who wanted to participate in sparring. They had to be able to take blows to the abdomen as effectively as any prizefighter. For that, they needed well-developed muscles.

actual sparring is the ultimate, and this training is only a means toward this.''

Besides running, Bruce also believed in exercises for the stomach, such as sit-ups and leg raises. "Too often one of those big-belly Chinese masters will tell you that his *chi* (internal power) was sunken to his stomach," Bruce quipped. "He's not kidding. It is sunken, and gone! To put it bluntly, he is nothing but fat and ugly."

Tools of the Trade

Bruce referred to his hands, feet, and body as the tools of the trade. The hands and feet must be sharpened and improved daily to be efficient. To illustrate this process, Bruce introduced some of his training equipment, which all martial artists could utilize.

One unique piece of training equipment Bruce found useful was the portable wooden dummy, which he brought over from Hong Kong—an improvement over the wing chun kung fu dummy. Bruce used the dummy, which was approximately six feet tall and 12 inches in diameter, to develop power and better techniques. Erected on an eight-foot-by-eight-foot platform, it was supported by a springy metal. The dummy had two portable hands below the neck and another in the center, which stretched out about two feet. The hands were constructed loosely and were removable. The dummy also had one metal leg that extended out and downward. Its hands were used to practice *pak sao* (blocking and punching) and *chi sao* (sticking hands) techniques.

Bruce admitted that the dummy would never replace a live sparring

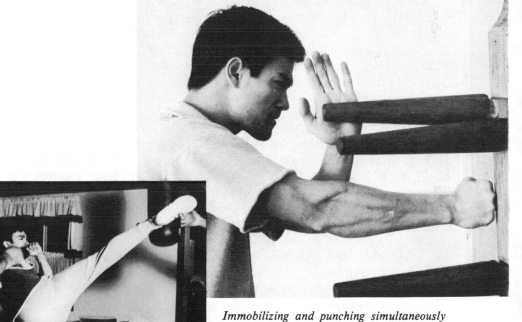

Immobilizing and punching simultaneously (above) is a common technique in jeet kune do, blurring the distinction between offense and defense. Another of Lee's favorite moves was the round kick (left) which he practiced on a small bag or a sheet of paper.

mate, but he still felt it was very useful. For pak sao, blocking and pulling techniques could be done with full force since the dummy could not be damaged. It was also useful in teaching one to punch straight. The dummy's foot was beneficial in teaching the martial artist to always place his front leg automatically to lock the opponent's leg, which prevented him from kicking. It is also valuable for practicing shin kicks.

Bruce used several different punching bags. The square wall bag filled with beans developed depth and penetration techniques. It also gave a feeling of hitting someone. Kicking techniques could also be applied to this piece of equipment.

The heavy, cotton-filled 70-pound boxing bag, which was used for both punching and kicking techniques, "is very valuable for my training in developing timing," Bruce said. "It teaches me to kick at the right moment and at the right distance to deliver the most powerful kick I can generate."

The heavy bag was also used to unleash heavy, continuous punches, keeping the opponent off balance and preventing him from recovering. The danger of training with the heavy bag, however, was that since it didn't react to an attack, a practitioner could become vulnerable in a real situation if he made a habit of punching the bag carelessly.

Power of the Punch

"The first rule," Bruce pointed out, "is to always keep yourself well covered at all times and never leave yourself open while sparring around the bag. By all means use your footwork: side-stepping, feinting, varying your kicks and blows to the bag. Do not shove or flick at it. Explode through it and remember that the power of the kick and punch come from the correct contact at the right spot and at the right moment with the body in perfect position, not from the vigor with which the kicks or blows are delivered, as many people think."

The olden-days speed bag, which was supported by a pair of springy cords, was also very functional, according to Bruce. It was useful in developing footwork and combination punches. In fact, he preferred it to the modern platform speed bag which only functions at a rhythmic-exercise instead of a timing-exercise apparatus. Since no one fights like that, Bruce insisted, the platform bag was only useful in sharpening the eyes and keeping the hands high.

"The olden-days punching speed bag teaches you to hit straight and square," Bruce explained. "If you don't hit it straight, the bag will not return directly to you. Besides teaching footwork, you can hit the bag upward, too. Another important function is that after the delivery of the

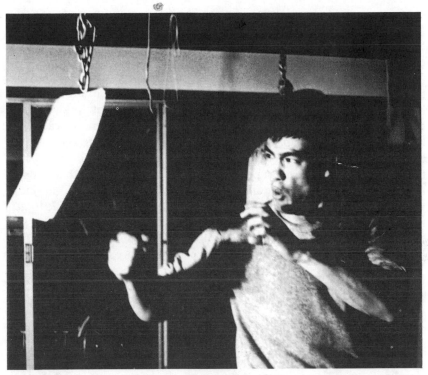

Punching a sheet of paper suspended from the ceiling was another Lee form of exercise which improved his lightning reflexes. It also helped in judging the proper distance for punching through a target, the secret of powerful punches.

punch the bag will return instantaneously, which teaches you to be alert and to recover quickly.''

Bruce advised that instead of a rhythmic motion the bag should be hit in a broken rhythm. "Actually fight the bag as if it is your opponent.''

Bruce used the round punching pad for perfecting all different types of punches and practicing his hook kick to the face. His partner couldn't control the height and distance as Bruce struck toward the moving target. The punching pad was an asset to conditioning and acquiring skill in punching. It taught one not to telegraph his punches.

The jabbing pad was used to increase speed in jabbing the opponent's eyes. It also taught one to jab without injuring his fingers. Bruce had shown his speed in many a karate tournament, and no one was able to block his thrust even when he was moving in from several feet away.

The paper target, a sheet of paper hung on a heavy rope or chain at any height, was used to help increase speed and correct application of the body for power. It helped develop his movement in punching and in both side and hook kicking. Another use of the paper target was that it taught proper distance.

To develop both proper distance and penetration against a moving target, Bruce used a partner either equipped with a body protector or an air bag. His partner could either stand still and take the brunt of the kick, or he could back away from the attack. The former teaches proper application of the kick, especially valuable in teaching beginners. The latter training was to teach penetration. As soon as the partner thought Bruce would attack, he tried to back away as fast as possible. This practice was valuable to both men; one learned to penetrate and the other to back away quickly. Many top karateka who worked out with Bruce attest that they were not able to get away from this simple attack.

The body protector was sometimes used for sharpening the attack. The partner did not attack but maintained a correct distance in a ready fighting

One of Bruce's favorite kicks was the side kick which he liked to practice on both the football blocking pad held by a partner and also on the heavy bag (70 pounds) which he thought of as his most important piece of equipment. Even with the heavy bag, a partner was needed to stop its swing. Here the impact of the kick really jolted his partner.

Bruce always supplemented his training on the wing chun dummy (left) with more advanced jeet kune do sparring with protective gear (below) stressing the realities of actual combat against a live opponent.

pose. As Bruce began to attack, the partner tried to counter, block, or move away. Bruce would almost have the actual feeling of hitting his opponent in a real situation.

Broken Rhythm

Free-style sparring with protective equipment headed the list on Bruce Lee's training schedule. "There is nothing better than free-style sparring in the practice of any combative art," Bruce maintained. "In sparring, you should wear suitable protective equipment and go all out. Then you can truly learn the correct timing and distance for the delivery of the kicks, punches, etc. It is a good idea to spar with all types of individuals: tall, short, fast, clumsy. Yes, at times a clumsy fellow would mess up a better man because his awkwardness served as a sort of broken rhythm. The best sparring partner, though, is a quick, strong man who does not know anything, a mad man who goes all out scratching, grabbing, punching, and kicking.

"To me, totality is very important in sparring. Many styles claim . . . they can cope with all types of attacks . . . (that) their structures cover all the possible lines and angles with the capacity to retaliate from all angles and lines. If this is true, then how did all the different styles come about? Also, if they are in totality, why do some use only the straight lines, others the round lines, some only kicks, and still others who want to be different just flap and flick their hands? To me, a system that clings to one small aspect of combat is actually in bondage.

"A martial artist who exclusively drills on a set pattern of combat is losing his freedom," Bruce continued. "He is actually becoming a slave to a choice pattern and feels that the pattern is the real thing. It leads to clogginess because the way of combat is never based on personal choice and fancies. Instead, it constantly changes from moment to moment, and the disappointed combatant will soon find out that his 'choice routine' lacks pliability. One must be free. Instead of complexity of form, it should be simplicity of expression. He should be alive in sparring, throwing punches and kicks from all angles, not a cooperative robot.

Often in practice or when demonstrating jeet kune do to the public, Lee and his partners wore protective equipment so they could be spontaneous and go all out.

Isometrics played an important part in Bruce Lee's training. Here, pressing up on a cross bar, he works his shoulders, chest, and back.

"Like water, it should be formless. Pour it into a cup, it becomes part of the cup. Pour it into a bottle, it becomes part of the bottle. Try to kick or punch it, it is resilient. Clutch it and it will yield without hesitation. In fact, it will escape as pressure is being applied to it. How true it is that nothingness cannot be confined. The softest thing cannot be snapped.

"Efficiency in sparring or fighting is not a matter of correct, classical, traditional form. Efficiency is anything that scores. Creating fancy forms and classical sets to replace sparring is like trying to wrap and tie a pound of water into the manageable shape of a paper sack. For something that is static, fixed, dead, there can be a way or a definite path, but not for anything that is moving and living. In sparring, there's no exact path or method but, instead, a perceptive, pliable, choiceless awareness. It lives from moment to moment.

"The idea of hard versus soft and internal versus external is not important. The yin and yang is in reality two halves of a whole. Each half is equally important and each is interdependent on the other. If one rejects either the firm or the gentle, this will lead to one extreme. Those who cling to either extreme are known as the physical-bound or the intellectual-bound. But the former are more bearable; at least in combat they do struggle."

Chapter 5

Liberate Yourself From Classical Karate

by Bruce Lee

A learned man once went to a Zen teacher to inquire about Zen. As the Zen teacher explained, the learned man would frequently interrupt him with remarks like, "Oh, yes, we have that too . . ." and so on.

Finally, the Zen teacher stopped talking and began to serve tea to the learned man. He poured the cup full, then kept pouring until the cup overflowed.

"Enough!" the learned man once more interrupted. "No more can go into the cup!"

"Indeed, I see," answered the Zen teacher. "If you do not first empty your cup, how can you taste my cup of tea?"

I hope my comrades in the martial arts will read the following paragraphs with open-mindedness, leaving all the burdens of preconceived opinions and conclusions behind. This act, by the way, has in itself a liberating power. After all, the usefulness of the cup is in its emptiness.

Make this article relate to yourself because, though it is on jeet kune do, it is primarily concerned with the blossoming of a martial artist—not a "Chinese" martial artist or a "Japanese" martial artist. A martial artist is a human being first. Just as nationalities have nothing to do with one's humanity, so they have nothing to do with the martial arts. Leave your protective shell of isolation and relate *directly* to what is being said. Return to your senses by ceasing all the intervening intellectual mumbo jumbo. Remember that life is a constant process of relating. Remember, too, that I seek neither your approval nor to influence you toward my way of thinking. I will be more than satisfied if, as a result of this article, you begin to investigate everything for yourself and cease to uncritically accept prescribed formulas that dictate "this is this" and "this is that."

On Choiceless Observation

Suppose several persons who are trained in different styles of combative arts witness an all-out streetfight. I am sure we would hear different versions from each of these stylists. Such variations are quite understandable, for one cannot see a fight (or anything else) "as is" as long as he is blinded by his chosen point of view, i.e. style, and he will view the fight through the lens of

Learning to be direct is an important part of jeet kune do. The finger jabs to the throat (right) and to the eyes (above) are applied with a simultaneous block of the opponent's technique.

his particular conditioning. Fighting, as is, is simple and total. It is not limited to your perspective or conditioning as a Chinese martial artists. True observation begins when one sheds set patterns, and true freedom of expression occurs when one is beyond systems.

Before we examine jeet kune do, let's consider exactly what a "classical" martial art style really is. To begin with, we must recognize the incontrovertible fact that regardless of their many colorful origins (by a wise, mysterious monk, by a special messenger in a dream, or in a holy revelation) styles are created by men. A style should never be considered gospel truth, the laws and principles of which can never be violated. Man, the living, creating individual, is always more important than any established style.

It is conceivable that a long time ago a certain martial artist discovered some partial truth. During his lifetime, the man resisted the temptation to organize this partial truth, although this is a common tendency in man's

Jeet kune do training is fundamentally similar to boxing in that it emphasizes flexible responses rather than preconceived movements. How to block a kick (left) is simple reflex, and when to execute a kick (below) is determined by what is needed at that instant. Wearing protective gear is useful in jeet kune do training because it allows contact (below left) without injury. Contact is very important for a better understanding of real combat.

search for security and certainty in life. After his death, his students took "his" hypothesis, "his" postulates, "his" inclination, and "his" method and turned them into law. Impressive creeds were then invented, solemn reinforcing ceremonies prescribed, rigid philosophy and patterns formulated, and so on, until finally an institution was erected. So what originated as one man's intuition of some sort of personal fluidity was transformed into solidified, fixed knowledge, complete with organized, classified responses presented in a logical order. In so doing, the well-meaning, loyal followers not only made this knowledge a holy shrine but also a tomb in which they buried the founder's wisdom.

But the distortion did not necessarily end here. In reaction to "the other's truth," another martial artist, or possibly a dissatisfied disciple, organized an opposite approach—such as the "soft" style versus the "hard" style, and "internal" school versus the "external" school, and all these separative nonsenses. Soon this opposite faction also became a large organization, with its own laws and patterns. A rivalry began, with each style claiming to possess the "truth" to the exclusion of all others.

At best, styles are merely parts dissected from a unitary whole. All styles require adjustment, partiality, denials, condemnation, and a lot of self-justification. The solutions they purport to provide are the very cause of the problem because they limit and interfere with our natural growth and obstruct the way to genuine understanding. Divisive by nature, styles keep men *apart* from each other rather than unite them.

Truth Cannot be Confined

One cannot express himself fully when imprisoned by a confining style. Combat "as is" is total, and it includes all the "is" as well as the "is not," without favorite lines or angles. Lacking boundaries, combat is always fresh, alive, and constantly changing. Your particular style, your personal inclinations, and your physical makeup are all *parts* of combat, but they do not constitute the *whole* of combat. Should your responses become dependent upon any single part, you will react in terms of what "should be" rather than to the reality of the ever-changing "what is." Remember that while the whole is evidenced in all its parts, an isolated part—efficient or not—does not constitute the whole.

Prolonged repetitious drillings will certainly yield mechanical precision and security of the kind that comes from any routine. However, it is exactly this kind of "selective" security, or "crutch," which limits or blocks the total growth of a martial artist. In fact, quite a few practitioners develop such a liking for and dependence on their "crutch" that they can no longer walk without it. Thus, any one special technique, however cleverly designed, is actually a hindrance.

Let it be understood once and for all that I have *not* invented a new style, composite, or modification. I have in no way set jeet kune do within a distinct form governed by laws that distinguish it from "this" style or "that" method. On the contrary, I hope to free my comrades from bondage to styles, patterns, and doctrines.

What, then, is jeet kune do? I am the first to admit that any attempt to crystalize jeet kune do into a written article is no easy task. Do remember, however that "jeet kune do" is merely a convenient name. I am not interested with the term itself; I am interested in its effect of liberation when JKD is used as a mirror for self-examination.

Unlike a "classical" martial art, there is no series of rules or classification of technique that constitutes a distinct jeet kune do method of fighting. JKD is not a form of special conditioning with its own rigid philosophy. It looks at combat not from a single angle, but from all possible angles. While JKD utilizes all ways and means to serve its end (after all, efficiency is anything that scores), it is bound by none and is therefore free. In other words, JKD possesses everything but is in itself possessed by nothing.

Therefore, to attempt to define JKD in terms of a distinct style—be it kung fu, karate, streetfighting, or Bruce Lee's martial art—is to completely miss its meaning. Its teaching simply cannot be confined within a system. Since JKD is at once "this" and "not this," it neither opposes nor adheres to any style. To understand this fully, one must transcend from the duality

Without preconceived ideas one is free to act more spontaneously.

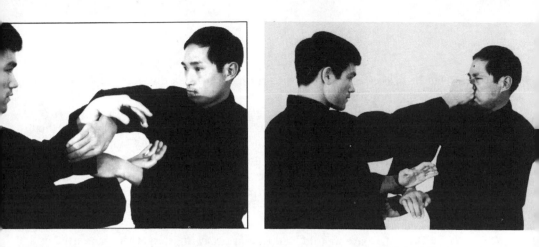

One must be ready to act without knowing what situation will present itself. Here (left), Ted Wong allows his wrists to cross. A quick but simple push downwards (right) traps both his hands together and leaves him open.

of "for" and "against" into one organic unity which is without distinctions. Understanding of JKD is direct intuition of this unity.

There are no prearranged sets or *kata* (forms) in the teaching of JKD, nor are they necessary. Consider the subtle difference between "having no form" and "have no form." The first is ignorance; the second is transcendence. Through instinctive body feeling, each of us *knows* our own most efficient and dynamic manner of achieving effective leverage, balance in motion, and economical use of energy. Patterns, techniques, or forms touch only the fringe of genuine understanding. The core of understanding lies in the individual mind, and until that is touched everything is uncertain and superficial. Truth cannot be perceived until we come to fully understand ourselves and our potentials. After all, *knowledge in the martial arts ultimately means self-knowledge.'*

At this point you may ask, "How do I gain this knowledge?" That you will have to find out all by yourself. You must accept the fact that there is no help but self-help. For the same reason I cannot tell you how to "gain" freedom, since freedom exists within you, I cannot tell you how to "gain" self-knowledge. While I can tell you what *not* to do, I cannot tell you what you *should* do, since that would be confining you to a particular approach. Formulas can only inhibit freedom; externally dictated prescriptions only squelch creativity and assure mediocrity. Bear in mind that the freedom that accures from self-knowledge cannot be acquired through strict adherence to a formula. We do not suddenly *become* free; we simply *are* free.

Learning is definitely not mere imitation, nor is it the ability to accumulate and regurgitate fixed knowledge. Learning is a constant process of discovery—a process without end. In JKD we begin not by accumulation but by discovering the cause of our ignorance—a discovery that involves a shedding process.

Unfortunately, most students in the martial arts are conformists. Instead of learning to depend on themselves for expression, they blindly follow their instructors, no longer feeling alone, and finding security in mass imitation. The product of this imitation is a dependent mind. Independent inquiry, which is essential to genuine understanding, is sacrificed. Look around the martial arts and witness the assortment of routine performers, trick artists, desensitized robots, glorifiers of the past, and so on—all followers or exponents of organized despair.

How often are we told by different *sensei* (masters) that the martial arts are life itself? But how many of them truly understand what they are saying? Life is a constant movement—rhythmic as well as random. Life is constant change, not stagnation. Instead of choicelessly flowing with this process of change, many of these "masters," past and present, have built an illusion of fixed forms, rigidly subscribing to traditional concepts and techniques of the art, solidifying the ever-flowing, dissecting the totality.

The most pitiful sight is to see sincere students earnestly repeating those imitative drills, listening to their own screams and spiritual yells. In most cases, the means these sensei offer their students are so elaborate that the students must give tremendous attention to them, until gradually they lose sight of the end. They end up performing their methodical routines as a mere conditioned response, rather than *responding to* "what is." They no longer

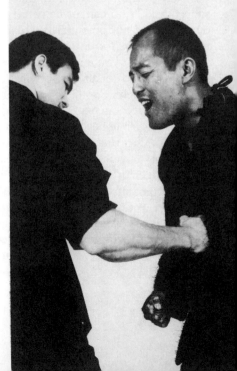

As shown here, penetrating power in punching techniques (right) as well as in kicks (above), is gained through economy of movement.

In jeet kune do, an unorthodox method such as this high kick in close quarters cannot be ruled out. It may be the best response to the situation at that instant.

listen to circumstances; they *recite* their circumstances. These poor souls have unwittingly become trapped in the miasma of classical martial arts training.

Pointing to the Truth

A teacher, a really good sensei, is never a *giver* of "truth," he is a guide, a *pioneer* to the truth that the student must discover for himself. A good teacher, therefore, studies each student individually and encourages the student to explore himself, both internally and externally, until, ultimately, the student is integrated with his being. A good teacher is a catalyst. Besides possessing deep understanding, he must also have a responsive mind with great flexibility and sensitivity.

There is no standard in total combat, and expression must be free. This liberating truth is a reality only in so far as it is *experienced and lived* by the individual himself; it is a truth that transcends styles or disciplines. Remember, too, that jeet kune do is merely a term, a label to be used as a boat to get one across; once across, it is to be discarded and not carried on one's back.

These few paragraphs are, at best, a "finger pointing to the moon." Please do not take the finger to be the moon or fix your gaze so intently on the finger as to miss all the beautiful sights of heaven. After all, the usefulness of the finger is in pointing away from itself to the light which illumines finger and all.

PART 3

Chapter 6

Super Star Bruce Lee: An Acclaimed Phenomenon

by Mike Plane

"The biggest disadvantage of success," said Bruce Lee, "is losing your privacy. It's ironic but we all strive to become wealthy and famous, but once you're there, it's not all rosy. There's hardly a place in Hong Kong where I can go to without being stared at or people asking for autographs. That's one reason I spend a lot of time at my house to do my work. Right now, my home and the office are the most peaceful places."

Lee avoided social gatherings whenever possible. "I'm not that kind of cat," he said. "I don't drink or smoke and those events are many times senseless. I don't like to wear stuffy clothes and be at places where everyone is trying to impress each other. Now, I'm not saying I'm modest. I rather like to be around a few friends and talk informally about such things as boxing and the martial arts.

"Whenever I have to go to public places like a restaurant, I try to sneak in without being detected. I'll go directly to a corner table and quickly sit down, facing the wall so my back is to the crowd. I keep my head low while eating. No, I'm not crazy," he laughed, "I only look like it. You see, if I'm recognized I'm dead, because I can't eat with the hand that I have to use to sign autographs. And I'm not one of those guys that can brush people off. Besides, I feel that if I can just take a second and make someone happy, why not do it."

Smiling, Lee explained that the Hong Kong fans could find you every-

In a scene from the movie Fists of Fury, *Bruce displays his flying side kick to an astonished adversary. This film, which was released in Hong Kong as* The Big Boss, *marked Bruce's first starring role in a feature film. Bruce, nicknamed "The Little Dragon," was an incredible phenomenon to watch. He received instant acclaim for his performance, first in Hong Kong, and then in the United States.*

where, even in the dark. "Once when I went to a movie, the usherette shined her flashlight into my face and asked for an autograph," he recalled.

"Now, I understand why stars like Steve (McQueen) and Big Louis (Kahrcem Jabbar) avoid public places. In the beginning," continued Lee, "I didn't mind all the publicity I was getting. But soon, it got to be a headache answering the same questions over and over again, posing for photos and forcing a smile."

I'm Free

Bruce liked to return to the U.S., "I find peace here. I'm free. I'm like anyone else here and can go to any place without being stopped. I like to return here and have myself another house." (Lee sold his Bel-Air home to live in Hong Kong.)

Is it a fluke that Bruce Lee was one of the biggest stars of his time? He didn't think so. "Maybe when I was hired to play Kato in *The Green Hornet*, it was an accident. I didn't have any acting experience." He had acted in Chinese films since he was a child but not in U.S. films. Lee had no contact in Hollywood. One year while giving an exhibition of kung fu at the Long Beach International Karate Championships (in California), a Hollywood producer just happened to be in the audience. "That night I received a phone call at my hotel for a tryout. Early next morning, I stopped by 20th Century-Fox and was hired to be Charlie Chan's new Number One Son. While attending a 'quickie' one month private crash course in acting, the producer changed his mind and decided that I would be Kato instead."

Lee explained that the reason for the change was because *Batman and Robin* had caught the fancy of the kids and *The Green Hornet* was a natural for television. The series ran for 30 weeks in the U.S.

Lee did not feel that his rise to stardom came strictly from luck. "Some martial artists are now going to Hong Kong to be in movies," he noticed, "they think they can be lucky, too. Well, I don't believe in pure luck," Lee said seriously. "You have to create your own luck. You have to be aware of the opportunities around you and take advantage of them. Some guys may not believe it, but I spent hours perfecting whatever I did.

"Nope, I'm not the type of guy who can sit in the office doing the same routine day in and day out," he continued. "I have to do something creative and interesting (to me). I don't want to do anything half way, it has to be perfect," he explained. "I feel that I want to be the best martial artist. Not just for the sake of movies but because this is my interest. To be good, I have to spend a lot of time practicing. My minimum daily training is two hours; this includes running three miles, special weight training, kicking and hitting the light and heavy bags.

"I really dig exercise," he beamed. "When I'm jogging early in the morning, boy! it's sure refreshing. Although Hong Kong is one of the most crowded places in the world, I'm surprised how peaceful it can be in the morning. Sure, there are people but I become oblivious to them while I am running."

Reasons for Success

Many think that Bruce Lee's success in Hong Kong came about because he was a "local product." Others feel that his rapid climb to stardom was due to *The Green Hornet* being played in Hong Kong repeatedly for months after it disappeared from the tube in the U.S. "I guess I'm the only guy who ventured away from there and became an actor. To most people, including the actors and actresses, Hollywood is like a magic kingdom. It's beyond everyone's reach and when I made it, they thought I'd accomplished an incredible feat. But if my success was based on these two facts alone, then why is it that *The Green Hornet* smashed box offices in Singapore, Philippines and other countries I haven't even visited?"

When Bruce Lee decided to visit his homeland in 1968, he was surprised to learn that he was a celebrity. From the time he stepped off the airplane, he was constantly surrounded and hounded by the reporters from newspapers and television. "It sure was an experience. I made several appearances with the

Following his role in The Green Hornet *as Kato (below left), co-starring with Van Williams (left), Bruce kept martial arts in the public eye by following up with another TV show,* Longstreet *with James Franciscus (below) in which he taught the true spirit behind martial arts.*

largest radio and television stations. People flocked around me wherever I went. Although I wasn't paid for these appearances, I was rewarded in other ways.''

After Lee left Hong Kong, the news media didn't forget him. They continued to follow his progress in the U.S. In the meantime Lee kept himself busy by teaching some Hollywood celebrities his style of fighting, jeet kune do. Some of his better-known students included Steve McQueen, James Coburn, Sterling Silliphant and Sy Weintraub. Because Lee didn't particularly like to teach, he charged a high fee.

Finally, Lee got his break. Paramount produced a TV series called *Longstreet* with James Franciscus in the starring role. Lee was invited as a guest star for the fourth segment of the episode, titled ''Way of the Fist.'' Because of his excellent performance with Franciscus the producer decided to debut the fall opener with Lee in it. The reviews from the trade papers and others like the *L.A.* and *N.Y. Times* were gratifying. ''First time in my life that I had any kind of review for my acting," said Lee, "I'm glad they were favorable."

While Lee was shooting *Longstreet,* the demand for his services were coming in heavily from Hong Kong and Taiwan. "After I left Hong Kong, the media there kept in contact with me through the telephone. Those guys used to call me early in the morning and even kept a conversation going on the air, so the public was listening to me.

"Then one day, the radio announcer asked me if I would do a movie there. When I replied that I would do it if the price was right, I began to get calls from producers in Hong Kong and Taiwan. Offers to do a movie varied from $2,000 to $10,000."

Lee finally signed up with Raymond Chow, producer of Golden Harvest in Hong Kong. "After I signed my contract with Raymond," he similed, "I received a call from a producer in Taiwan. That guy told me to rip up the contract and he'd top Raymond's offer and even take care of any lawsuit for breaking the agreement."

The Big Boss

The young man refused to break the contract. In July of 1971, he traveled to a small town in the outskirts of Bangkok, Thailand. "When I signed to do *The Big Boss* (Lee's first movie) I had a voice in it. Fortunately, I had some background in U.S. filming technique. We had quite a bit more sophisticated styles than they did and with my experience, I was able to help them, especially choreographing the fight scene."

Lee actually talked Chow into doing a martial arts film with only a minimum use of weapons. Up to then, the Chinese films attempted to emulate the Japanese samurai movies and the use of swords was heavily emphasized. With Bruce Lee's expertise in the martial arts and with his knowledge of film production, *The Big Boss* (played in the U.S. as *Fists of Fury*) broke all records in Hong Kong. It grossed $3.2 million (Hong Kong), surpassing *Sound of Music*, which held the record for a number of years at $2.8 million (H.K.). Lee's first movie began to break records in other countries like the Philippines, Singapore, Malaysia, etc. Movie critics raved about Lee and mentioned that *The Big Boss* would hold the record for many years to come or that it may never be broken.

"*The Big Boss* was an important movie for me because I had a starring role for the first time," said Lee. "I felt that I could do a better acting job than in *The Green Hornet* and had more confidence since I just did Paramount's TV movie *Way of the Fist*. I didn't expect *Big Boss* to break any kind of record but I did expect it to be a money maker. I realized the potential of the movie when I attended the premiere.

"Bob Baker (from Stockton) was in town for a part in the second movie, *Fists of Fury*. He and I sat in the front seats without being noticed. As the movie progressed, we kept looking at the reactions of the fans. They hardly made any noise in the beginning but at the end they were in a frenzy and began clapping and clamoring. Those fans there are emotional. If they don't like the movie, they'll cuss and walk out. When the movie came to an end, Bob, almost in tears, shook my hand and said, 'Boy, am I happy for you.' "

While Lee was shooting *The Big Boss*, Paramount was desperately looking for him after the fall opener. "They couldn't get to me because I really was in the sticks. We were so far out that we couldn't even get meat. I had only vegetables and rice and lost ten pounds."

Paramount wanted Lee to do three more segments of *Longstreet*. "It's funny but when Paramount sent telegrams and telephoned Hong Kong for

Hopelessly outnumbered in Enter the Dragon, *Lee nevertheless manages to keep the villain's cowardly henchmen at bay with a pair of kali sticks.*

In Way of the Dragon *Lee uses a pair of nunchaku to drive off a group of thugs. Here he finishes off an attacker without looking.*

me, boy, the producers thought I was an important star. My prestige must have increased three times," he chuckled.

When the muscular Lee came back for the three segments with Paramount, *The Big Boss* was already breaking records. "Paramount wanted me to be a regular for *Longstreet* but I refused because I was getting offers from Warner Bros. and MGM. Besides, I still had another commitment with Raymond Chow."

A year before *The Big Boss*, Lee already had a premonition that he was going to become a star, not only in the Far East but around the world. He told one prõducer that he expected to follow the steps of Charles Bronson and Clint Eastwood (both men became stars when they went to Europe) but Lee would do it in the Far East. The producer told him that because he was an Oriental, it would not be possible. The American and the European fans would not accept him.

The young star did not argue nor attempt to prove him wrong. "Deep inside, I knew I could do it," said Lee. "This is why I didn't sign a long contract with any of the major movie studios."

When his second movie hit the theaters, Bruce Lee became a bigger box-office draw. He made a lot of movie critics "eat their words" because *Fists of Fury* (played in the U.S. as *The Chinese Connection*) outgrossed *The Big*

Boss. It amassed $4.5 million (H.K.) and recorded a bigger gain in other countries. In the Philippines it ran for over six months capacity, and the government finally had to limit the amount of foreign film imports to protect their domestic film producers.

In Singapore, scalpers were getting $45.00 for a $2.00 ticket. On opening night, hundreds of movie patrons rushed to the theater and caused such a traffic jam that they had to suspend showing the movie for a week until the authorities found a way to resolve the problem. This was the first time in Singapore history that a movie caused such a jam.

Lee had already developed a precedent. When other producers began to lose money, they offered Lee fabulous amounts. They made their offers known directly in the newspaper headlines. "I had a heck of a problem after my second movie became a smash," said Lee. "I had people stop by at my door and just pass me a check for $200,000. When I asked them what it was for they replied, 'Don't worry about it, it's just a gift to you.' I didn't even know these people, they were strangers to me."

Confused With Offers

The five-foot, seven-inch star said he became confused with all the offers and he began to become suspicious of everyone. "It was very bewildering. I didn't know who to trust and I even grew suspicious of my old pals. I was in a period when I didn't know who was trying to take advantage of me.

"When people just pass out big money—just like that," continued the wiry star, "you don't know what to think. I destroyed all those checks but it was difficult to do, because I didn't know what they were for."

After his second movie, Bruce Lee formed his own production company, Concorde. He took in Raymond Chow as his partner and they produced their first movie called *Way of the Dragon.* Lee felt that *The Big Boss* was an important movie, because with it he got his break as a star, but he placed *Way of the Dragon* above his first two movies in importance. "In *Way of the Dragon* I wrote the script, had the starring role, directed it and produced it. I worked almost around the clock for days and lost several more pounds. I did it because it was fun. It was something I hadn't done before but always had an interest in. I got hold of a dozen books on film production and direction and really dug into them."

When the superstar predicted that *Way of the Dragon* would surpass a $5-million take in Hong Kong, the movie critics really thought that Bruce had gone overboard. "How could a movie outgross *Sound of Music* by almost two times?" they asked.

When *Way of the Dragon* completed its run in Hong Kong, it established

a new record, $5.4 million. The new producer predicted it correctly again. "*Way of the Dragon* was different from the other movies," described Bruce. "We went to Europe for location. The fight scenes between Chuck (Norris) and me were held in the Colosseum in Rome. I also employed a Japanese photographer because I knew the Japanese had more know-how in that area than those in Hong Kong. This was the first time a Hong Kong filmmaker went to Europe for location shooting.

"The movie was a little more costly from a Hong Kong standard but we got our returns right away," continued Lee. "Before it even opened, we already sold the distribution rights to Taiwan for the whole production cost."

Too Far Out for the Americans

Although his first two movies played in the U.S., Lee was not planning to release his *Way of the Dragon* here. "The three movies I made," said Lee,

For Enter the Dragon *Bruce Lee choreographed a magnificent fight scene. Face to face at last with his mortal enemy, Han, Bruce uses a variety of martial arts techniques. A round kick to the head (left) sends Han stumbling back. Then, after being cut by Han's knives (below), Lee brings him down by trapping one leg and sweeping the other.*

"were not intended for the audience in the U.S. They were strictly for the Far East. I had no control over the first two. They are too far out for the Americans. I'm surprised though, they brought in a lot of money for the distributors."

Lee felt that one day he was going to be an international star. *Enter the Dragon* (produced by Warner Bros. and Lee's Concorde) should make it," he smiled proudly. "This is the movie that I'm proud of because it is made for the U.S. audience as well as for the European and Oriental. This is definitely the biggest movie I ever made. I'm excited to see what will happen. I think it's going to gross $20 million in the U.S."

Enter the Dragon was the most expensive production Lee had participated in. Producers Fred Weintraub and Paul Heller thought like Lee, that it was going to be the highest grossing martial arts movie ever made. Lee, who portrayed a James Bond-type of secret agent, had an excellent supporting cast including veteran star John Saxon, actress Ahna Capri, Jim Kelly (of *Melinda*) and Bob Wall. The latter two were veteran karatemen.

The James Bone-type movie was directed by Bob Clouse, an Academy Award nominee. All the fight scenes were choreographed by Bruce Lee. The music was composed by Lalo Schifrin.

Money was an important item to Bruce but he placed his family before that. "I like to have my children (son Brandon and daughter Shannon) educated here. They are attending the same parochial school I did. But then, how important is school?" he queried. "I barely made passing grades while attending the University of Washington."

Wished to Live in the U.S.

Linda, Lee's wife, wanted to live in the U.S. "Hong Kong is too hard for kids. It's crowded and I don't like to have them being exposed to all the publicity. I want to raise them as normal kids."

What was in store for Lee's future? He had been offered two movies in Hungary which he expected to work in. According to reliable sources, the offer he got made him the highest paid actor in the world. Warner Bros. also negotiated to do several movies with him. "He's in an enviable position," explained a producer. "He could do movies in Europe, the U.S., or the Orient. Since he owns his own production company, he doesn't have to wait around for a job like the rest of the actors."

Executed against Chuck Norris in Way of the Dragon, *one of Lee's favorite techniques in his cinema fights was the leg sweep which showed off his great quickness.*

The Chinese Connection's final shot has its hero played by Lee charging his enemies, choosing to die rather than be punished as an example to his oppressed countrymen.

In two years, Lee's style of living changed rapidly. He owned an 11-bedroom mansion with a college-size gym. He had three servants and three maids to maintain it. He ordered a special Rolls Royce which he expected to be delivered from England. "Nope, I don't expect to use a chauffeur," he beamed. "I can't see myself sitting in the back seat of a car. Yep, I expect to drive it myself.

"Having money doesn't solve all of your problems," he explained, "but it sure beats not having money. I think I could have made a fortune a few years ago when *The Green Hornet* was playing. I was approached by several businessmen to open a franchise of Kato's Self-Defense School throughout the U.S., but I refused. I felt then and still feel that I'm not going to prostitute the art for the sake of money. I don't want people to say that they studied under me when they didn't."

It is not unusual to hear of actors or actresses reaching stardom, but it is unusual for an Oriental actor to reach the pinnacle in the world of make-believe. Bruce Lee was the only one who did it.

Chapter 7

Date With Destiny: Bruce Lee, Raymond Chow, Lo Wei

by Mike Plane

Call it mysticism, magic or coincidence of timing, but the strange chemical elements that caused three people of rather diverse backgrounds to converge for the first time in a small Thailand village not far from Bangkok served to create a phenomenon in the world history of entertainment.

Hong Kong director Lo Wei had replaced the original director on a Golden Harvest production there. He was met by producer Raymond Chow, who had flown in from Hong Kong to personally supervise the production of his film, then called *The Big Boss*. The two had been reshooting for about a week, working around the film's star—a young Chinese-American actor neither had ever met. The arrival of the star, Bruce Lee, had the effect of synergizing the whole chemistry of the making of the film. He inspired the company, and like the chemical process he enhanced the total effect.

From time to time each has been credited with the discovery of the others. In fact, each was well established. Yet, there is a certain almost mystical quality in their mutual appointment with destiny in that tiny, dirty

Fists of Fury *gave full range to Bruce's talents as an actor.*

Thai village. The magic they wrought catapulted Bruce Lee into the ranks of superstardom. The film, released in the English speaking world as *Fists of Fury* had not only broken box office records wherever it was shown, it created a wave of kung fu films that overwhelmed the whole entertainment industry.

The charismatic personality of Bruce Lee had full range. His mastery of the martial arts was superbly demonstrated. He choreographed his own work and set all of the fight scenes. His contribution to the film was in much

All the characters Bruce played on the screen seemed to have in common the dilemma of having to sublimate their intense feelings. Then, when circumstances demand it, these characters explode into action.

greater capacity than that of an actor, for he ended functioning as co-director and co-author.

The three men quickly made *Fists of Fury*, released in the U.S. as *The Chinese Connection*. Bruce took over directing chores for the next one, *Way of the Dragon*. The company formed by Raymond Chow and Bruce Lee, Concorde, then co-produced *Enter the Dragon* with Sequoia Productions and Warner Bros.

At the time of his death, Bruce was in the midst of *Game of Death*, a film he was directing, co-writing and starring in for Concorde and Golden Harvest.

Chapter 8

"Way of the Dragon" From the Beginning

by Linda Lee

I am trying to remember back now to the time when Bruce was preparing to go into his third feature film as a star. This is the film which was to be *Way of the Dragon*. He had just finished *Fists of Fury*, which, here, of course, was called *The Chinese Connection*. (Previously, he had made *The Big Boss,* released in this country as *Fists of Fury*.)

Bruce had been under contract to Golden Harvest for those first two films. That contract was completed; so he was on his own to negotiate new terms for his third picture. The great success of *Boss* and *Fury* made Bruce keenly aware that he must make a picture that would merit a greater public response, and at the same time, command even more respect and attention in the martial arts world.

There had been a long, hard struggle for Bruce to become successful in films. He knew for sure that it was hard and difficult to remain successful; so he had to work harder than he did during the time he was on his way up.

Golden Harvest had a script that Bruce was seriously considering doing. It was *The Yellow Faced Tiger,* subsequently produced starring another Chinese actor, Don Wang. (Dan Ivan and Chuck Norris also appeared in it.) Bruce had already had costume fittings for the picture before he decided he just couldn't do it at that time.

For Bruce, it was really a time of decision. He had to decide about his personal statement and commitment to kung fu feature films. Bruce was never satisfied with just riding along on success. Each film would have to top its predecessor. And he felt he could best realize this in his films if he had more control over all the elements of production.

Director/Writer

In Chinese movies, the director usually writes the script. A director in Hong Kong works from a scenario, kind of an outline, rather than a completed script. At the start, the script is in a pretty rough form. This allows the director to improvise according to the inspiration of the moment or the

Bruce worked closely with his actors to make sure each detail was carefully planned. They block out a scene (left) for the cameraman. Between takes (above) Bruce talks with an actor.

87

situation. That's what intrigued Bruce. So for feature number three, Bruce insisted that the script be finished before they started shooting. There were many meetings on the shaping of the script of *Yellow Faced Tiger* and Bruce and director Lo Wei could not come to final agreements on the details, so Bruce bowed out and decided to do something on his own.

Generally, Bruce was dissatisfied with the way films were made in Hong Kong. Of course, his exposure to filmmaking in the United States had a lot to do with shaping his thinking. He was very intelligent, had learned a lot and he had other offers coming in. So Bruce could afford to take the time to make the right decision.

Bruce bought a lot of books about filmmaking and brushed up on behind-the-scenes techniques. He felt there wasn't any "soul" in Chinese movies, that they just were running them off the assembly line and that was not what he wanted to do. He wanted to put his own stamp on each film that he did so it would be his own highly personalized statement of kung fu feature films. He wanted to be sure you would know it was a Bruce Lee film when you went to see it, and not just another chop-suey flick or another fighting movie or action movie—his would be something special.

Generally, there is a lack of material—or there was at that time—a lack of scripts of interest to Bruce. He had a growing realization that if he wanted to control all the elements of production, he would have to direct the script himself.

The script was another problem, but not a big one. Bruce was always thinking up ideas for movies. For years he'd been working out scenes that he was sure would be ideal to make a story better. So he decided, on pure guts, to write, direct, produce and star—to really do the whole thing himself— which was really a gutsy thing to do.

Once he made that decision, he knew he had the determination and dedication to make it work. He did worry about the reaction from his colleagues, but he was on the cresting wave of success. They were all eager for Bruce to do another film, and they wanted to work with him in it. I don't believe Bruce ever worried about the outcome of the film. He assumed full responsibility and plunged into work like a man possessed.

One reason behind Bruce's decision was a burning desire to give each character he played in each film a distinctively different personality. He realized that people came to see him as a fighter, but his characters had to have great depth, to have an individual personality worth something and to be able to fight, too.

No other actor in Hong Kong had ever taken the step Bruce was making at the beginnning of *Way*. None had ever written, directed and starred in their own film, much less functioned as a co-producer with real executive decisions and responsibilities.

It is interesting to note that Bruce refused to conform to the system of filmmaking in Hong Kong, just as he refused to conform to any one system in the martial arts.

Pre-Production

Bruce hit on the main idea of the script and then the development of it took place over many weeks of discussion and time spent alone going over and over the central idea and expanding it. He made trips to location sites that he thought about. He had many hours of discussion with the assistant director, Chih-yao Chang. They met at our house and spent hours at a time discussing the script and how it would be shot. I sat in on most of this, but the meetings were all conducted in Chinese so I didn't contribute much to this part of it. Sometimes Bruce and I would discuss it in English when we were alone, and I think just by talking about it a lot, Bruce was able to develop it into a more complete story. When he got to the actual production

Playing it cool in Enter the Dragon *(right), Bruce Lee requests the company of the woman who once used a certain dart. In* Way of the Dragon *(above) he shows his other side. Playing the polite young Tang Lung, he decides to take some action against one of the gang members threatening his friends.*

he knew what would play—what would work.

To Bruce, the making of a film was always a marriage of art and commercialism. Some people believe more one way, some another. Bruce thought it should be a perfect blend. If you got too artistic, you wouldn't draw a big box office, and if you were too commercial, you would betray yourself as an artist.

Bringing Chuck Norris and Bob Wall over to Hong Kong and Italy to participate in the film was both an aesthetic decision as well as a commercial one.

The commercial aspect of it was that in Hong Kong, and in fact, in most Southeast Asia where the major population is Chinese, they like to see their Chinese heroes conquering people of a different race. That sounds like racial prejudice. In fact, it is; but in view of Chinese history, it's understandable.

Lee and Norris work out a gesture for Norris' character. Though Norris plays Lee's enemy in the film, he is portrayed as a man of honor.

Exchanging kicks in their final fight in the Colosseum, Norris attempts a side kick (right) which Lee blocks. The fight takes the form of a supreme test of skill for both fighters. Tentatively they feel each other out at first. Later, Lee lands a round kick to the head (above).

Then, too, Chuck Norris had won several grand championship titles, and was a world-famous karateka. Bob Wall's credits were equally impressive. But just as important was what they would add aesthetically to the picture. Bruce wanted to fight with professional fighters rather than with actors or dancers. Bruce knew this type of professional fighting would give the film added tension, authenticity and genuineness. Bruce was more than satisfied with Chuck's and Bob's performances in the film—in their acting ability as well as in their fighting ability. Bob looked like such a bad guy that Warner Bros. and Sequoia cast him as a villain in *Enter the Dragon* after seeing his work in *Way of the Dragon*.

One big difficulty was in finding Caucasians to play the parts of villains. There were about ten Caucasians in the picture, and for a Chinese film, that's an unusually large number. The film was set in Rome, so there had to be Caucasians; but the portion of the film they were in was shot in Hong Kong, so they had to be from Hong Kong. There are very few Caucasian actors there. I think you'd have to look hard to find one full-time Caucasian actor in Hong Kong. Most do it as a hobby.

Jon Benn is actually a Hong Kong businessman, and he did very well in his role as the boss of the gang.

One reason they went to Rome for their location work is because Raymond Chow, Bruce's partner, had a contact there who could arrange for equipment, locations and the production details. You can see what an ambitious project it was becoming for a first-time director-writer-producer-actor to immerse himself in.

Another reason for going to Rome was that Bruce was attracted by the idea of fighting a duel in the Colosseum. That fight with Chuck is a climactic moment in the film, and the end is particularly touching.

When in Rome

There were some problems filming in Rome. They went there to start the film. No shooting had been done in Hong Kong. So they had to be really sure they could match their work in Hong Kong. Most of the people didn't have international passports or working visas, so they could only stay a maximum of three weeks. Special permission was granted for them. And there had to be a permit obtained for them to shoot in the Colosseum. Well, all the administration and logistics took time. And they were under extreme pressure to finish their shooting in three weeks and leave.

All of this gives the film what can be called a real *cinema verite* style. They shot on the streets, at the airport, and around Rome during traffic rush hours, pedestrian and tourist interference, and even some bad weather. I remember Bruce said once they had to shoot somewhere between 45 and 60 setups inside of the Rome airport in just one day. I remember him saying that he got broken into the rigors of location directing, as well as directing in general, very quickly.

Bruce demanded perfection of himself, and of everyone around him. I'm sure some thought he was very difficult to work with, but he knew what he wanted and he knew how to get it. He wasn't difficult in the way that he would get mad at people or anything like that. He didn't lose his temper. In fact, he was very patient with other actors and with the crew. If something wasn't right he just did it again and again until he was satisfied with it.

The schedule was stiff. They worked from 12 to 14 hours a day, and that was for seven days a week.

Of course, it got even worse for Bruce in Hong Kong. Part of the Hong

Kong director's responsibility was to supervise the setting up of shots for the next day's shooting. It was exhausting work, but he never let up. I never noticed a letdown of his enthusiasm for the project even after it was in release.

Choreographing the Fights

Staging the fight scenes was Bruce's specialty. They had to be super perfect. Each fight was planned on paper, each movement, each angle. For instance, the last big duel with Chuck Norris takes up 20 pages of written instructions on how it had to be done. It was all worked out ahead of time just like a dance number, just as carefully choreographed. Bruce worked it out at

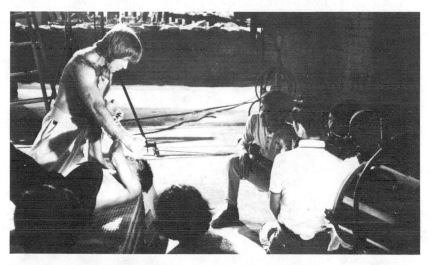

To capture the tension of the moment, Bruce directs his crew to shoot a close-up. Norris and Lee fight in close quarters in a test of wills.

home first in our study, usually with me because I happened to be the handiest one around. He would get a sudden inspiration or some idea would jell, and he's say, "Come on, let's try this." And we would try all the movements and then he'd quickly write it all down. And then we'd try something, and it wouldn't work, because of course, everything had to really work. It couldn't be just movement or show, just flash. So we tried for how it worked, how it looked and to see what the best angle to shoot the sequence would be. Bruce was always involved with thinking about new techniques because each fight had to be different from other fights in the film and also from his previous films.

Fight scenarios were really fascinating to Bruce. In the three films he did, including *Way of the Dragon,* there must have been about 30 fights. Each had to be different and had to fit into the character's personality. Then, too, when it was all planned in his head, and put down on paper, he knew exactly how it would go and how it would work for him. But then this had to be revised and carefully worked out for his opponent. Each had a different style, and a different physical size and strength. That always made a big difference. So those things had to be worked out. Bruce also wanted to use the talent the other fighter would bring to the occasion. So I don't want to give an erroneous impression that he had it all locked in before the other fighter or actor rehearsed with him.

In *Way of the Dragon*, he used a couple of weapons not used in his other films. He used a staff in one fight. And in another he used two nunchaku in-

In his back-alley training area, Bruce puts away one of his attackers with a backward swipe of his staff. He was expert with a variety of weapons.

Brandishing a pair of nunchaku (above) Bruce confronts another of the gang members sent to close down his friends' restaurant. Stepping in (right) with lightning speed, Bruce sends his opponent down.

stead of one. He uses the nunchaku against different weapons like a staff, a club or a knife. And he also made and used darts.

It was interesting the way Bruce resolved the problem of guns in this picture, because guns are part of the contemporary scene and it was only natural that they would come into the film.

In the use of the weapons and in staging the fight scenes with the Caucasian actors—except for Chuck Norris and Bob Wall—there were many problems because they were only part-time actors to begin with, and they didn't know the martial arts. The way Bruce resolved the problem was by concentrating on their reactions. When they were hit, they had carefully choreographed reactions.

You must remember that in a film you don't really hit the other guy, you come very close and the other person reacts as if they were hit. It takes care-

One of the chief thrills of Way of the Dragon *was Bruce resorting to his pair of nun-chaku which he usually kept tucked in his belt.*

ful timing and rehearsing. The fighters have to be very loose, so that the head snaps when it is apparently hit. They did a lot of exercises to loosen the neck and shoulders. And carrying that on, they had to be able to let the whole body go and just collapse. For some, it was hard because they weren't all that athletic; some were not in the best of physical condition. Those are pretty essential elements to any fight scenes or stunt work.

Bruce was very relieved when those parts of the film were finished and he could work with real martial artists like Chuck Norris, Bob Wall and Huang Jen Chih. That was no snap either because the fight had to be worked out for the camera angle so that it would look real. Bruce saw the dailies every day, and if there was any suggestion of a miss, the scene had to be done over again. It is difficult to choreograph because as the fight moves around the body positions and the arms can't block off or mask the action from the camera.

People often ask about his training of jeet kune do for work in the films. He never taught jeet kune do to actors for use in picture work. Bruce's martial arts performances for the screen, his choreography and his direction of other actors or martial artists is a skilled art, but it is not the kind of martial art one uses in sports or in a defense situation.

Censorship

When *Way of the Dragon* was finally ready for release in Hong Kong, it had to be submitted for censorship. It was released at the same time that an anti-violence campaign got under way there. The censors insisted that a scene—a small section of one—be cut. It's the one where Bruce lands about five quick consecutive kicks to Chuck's head. It was a beautiful movement, and it is included in the version released here.

One thing that is particularly noteworthy about the big duel between Bruce and Chuck is the way in which the viewer is led into the psychology of the fight and how that one fight alone represents true art with exceptionally beautiful movements coupled with the innate sense of combat and finally, violence.

All Hong Kong films are dubbed, that is, re-recorded in a dubbing studio because they are not shot with sound. There is just too much noise in Hong

Putting the opposition out of business seemed like something Bruce did every day of life. Here, actress Nora Miao, who co-stars with Bruce, tries to stay out of the way as he dispatches one more thug.

Kong to make sense out of recorded-on-the-scene sound; the population is one of the densest in the world. And the studios are not usually that sound-proof for daytime recording. So the dialogue is done at night after the film is finished. They are quite expert in Hong Kong at doing this. Bruce supervised all of the dubbing because that was such an important part of the film. The acting in dubbing sessions is just as important as the on-camera work. He didn't dub his own voice because he didn't speak Mandarin. And the English voice isn't his either, but it's very close. But the fighting sounds are Bruce's own.

There was an unusual incident when the music was recorded. Most Chinese films use available canned music in their scores. But this one had its

Chuck and Bruce rehearse the choreography for the Colosseum duel (left) as the crew stands by to film the action. Such careful rehearsal made it possible for them to make the action appear even more realistic. When Bruce lands a kick to Chuck's midsection (below), it really looks as though the kick is landing with full impact.

own special score composed, another first for one of Bruce's films. During the recording session, he sat in and played one of the percussion instruments.

Bruce, the Man in Charge

There wasn't one aspect of the film that Bruce didn't participate in. He supervised everything, drawing plans for sets, building of sets, choosing costumes, and finally, editing the film. I think he must have seen the film hundreds of times. I saw it at least 25 times in bits and pieces, and I'm sure I've seen the finished film more than that. I went along to watch the dailies, and also saw all the rough cuts. They worked first in black and white to check, but for actual editing Bruce insisted on a color print to be sure he had matching quality control of all printing.

Bruce's idea in making this film was to show another side of himself to Hong Kong audiences. I say Hong Kong because when this picture was planned and produced, it was intended for distribution only in Southeast Asia—in the established Hong Kong film markets. That was Bruce's original idea. He did not intend it for world distribution at all. So he aimed it at the Chinese audiences. He constructed and produced a story that he knew would appeal to the Chinese people. Of course, it does have an international flavor. He felt that this bit of sophistication would appeal to everyone, too.

He also planned on a very appealing character, that of Tang Lung, a naive country boy trying to adjust to situations in a crowded foreign capital. Through this character, Bruce was able to show a very humorous light side of himself that had not been previously apparent in his films. I think he drew a great deal from his own personal experiences in creating the character. Bruce was born here in San Francisco, but he grew up in Hong Kong. He came back when he was 18. He could speak some English, but it was very awkward for him. And he knew nothing about American customs, I think he remembered all of that when he did *Way of the Dragon*, and you'll see a lot of the real Bruce Lee personality in this picture, as well as his character.

One scene I enjoy a lot is when Bruce is sulking in one situation. He has been insulted by some of his Chinese co-workers. There is a closeup of Bruce and in the shot his expression, his look, is so much like our son Brandon that it's amazing. I've seen them both have that look so many times.

In *Way of the Dragon*, there are many distinctively Chinese touches and gestures that are more meaningful to the Chinese than to the Americans. Bruce knew he was appealing more directly to the vast Chinese population more than any other. He had many discussions with Raymond Chow and with Warner Bros. here about distributing *Way of the Dragon* internationally. Bruce had some very strong doubts about an international market, because he felt that dubbing it wouldn't be true to what the film was about. The country boy goes to Italy, but the dialogue there is done in English and Chinese because much of the action centers around the Chinese restaurant and the girl's apartment. So dubbing all of it in English would dilute the point of his not being able to understand much of the threats or actions leading up to the fights.

At the time Bruce died, world distribution was not under discussion, but I believe he had pretty much decided that it was a good thing to distribute it throughout the rest of the world. He had not come to a decision about having it with subtitles or dubbed in English.

Building up to the climax, the conflict intensifies in Way of the Dragon *as Lee gives a final warning to the chief villain. The villain responds by hiring specialists, including Chuck Norris and Bob Wall, to deal with Lee.*

Bruce made a wager that *Way of the Dragon* would be the top grosser in Hong Kong. So much rode on it for him that as the release came, and it began to rack up big box office grosses, Bruce's excitement and enthusiasm seemed to grow. Previously, *Fists of Fury* and *The Chinese Connection* had set records. Bruce bet that *Way of the Dragon* would top $5 million in Hong Kong dollars in the market. Nobody would believe it. But it got around, and into print. So the press challenged Bruce to tease him over his boasting. The fun mounted as the weeks went by. First one, then two and then over four million. Finally it went over the $5-million figure and smashed all records. He was delighted, of course, because it was a tribute to his achievements and his judgment in fashioning the film as he did. I wish he could have seen what *Enter the Dragon* did here.

I've seen this picture *Way of the Dragon* over and over. It's a funny thing that this film, more than any other films he made, is the one I never get tired of looking at.

Chapter 9

"Enter the Dragon"

by Steve Jacques

Film historians may well say that *Enter the Dragon* marked a precedent-breaking cooperative effort between Hollywood and Hong Kong film makers as significant as the East-West rapprochement between the U.S. and The People's Republic of China.

It seemed to be much more economically significant than the openings in the bamboo and dollar curtains pierced by ping pong. *Enter the Dragon* was the first joint effort by American and Oriental moviemakers in Hong Kong to co-produce a big budget major production. Warner Bros. and Sequoia Pictures, in association with Concorde Productions of Hong Kong, joined forces to put together the most ambitious Technicolor and Panavision effort filmed in the Orient. *Enter the Dragon* was an action picture dealing with the philosophy and mastery of the phenomenally popular martial arts, specifically karate and kung fu.

In a room full of mirrors, Han hides in ambush as Lee comes face to face with his own image surrounding him on all sides.

Bruce Lee and actor Yang Sze work out a fight scene. Yang Sze plays Han's chief henchman and assassin who is responsible for discipline on the island. As the story builds to its climax, John Saxon and Yang Sze fight to the death.

Two of the screen's most exciting and skilled stars, each representatives of their cultures, joined forces in the film. Bruce Lee, already Asia's reigning superstar whose films outgrossed *The Godfather* and *Sound of Music* in the Far East was considered the single factor in bringing the martial arts to its peak of worldwide popularity. The actor's unmatchable combination of fantastic physical strength and agility, finely chiseled good looks, and sensitive but powerfully projected talent made it obvious why this dynamic performer was now a major screen personality with American audiences. Only a film of the magnitude of *Enter the Dragon* could do him justice.

Lee's dramatic and often volatile personality marked him as a man to be reckoned with, not only by his on-screen adversaries but by producers intent on investing in one of tomorrow's superstars.

John Saxon, a major American film and television actor, co-starred with Lee. For the first time Saxon revealed on screen his more than 15 years of martial arts training. So demanding was Saxon's role in the film that the actor considered it the challenge of his career.

Together, these two modern-day Marco Polos top-lined a film that dispelled the "east is east and west is west" myth.

The first big budget martial arts film was five months on location with some of Hollywood's and Hong Kong's finest cinema technicians. Shot in Panavision and Technicolor, the film was on difficult location in Hong Kong for 13 grueling weeks that resulted in some of the most exciting and exacting fighting action ever filmed. *Enter the Dragon* was perhaps one of the most dangerous movies ever made because it depicted the most deadly hand-to-hand fights.

This film employed a variety of deadly martial arts' karate styles and kung fu. These martial arts are still the most skillful and lethal forms of fighting. An expert martial artist is one of the world's most efficient fighting machines.

The fundamentals of the martial arts as they are known today were developed in ancient China by Taoist and Buddhist monks who sought to protect their monasteries from the onslaught of invading bandits, government troops and even rival monks.

Highly disciplined in all phases of their life-style, the monks gradually refined the martial arts to a point of physical perfection. It took several centuries and the degree of intense concentrated dedication required for their true mastery to become an entire way of life. The martial arts deserve to be

John Saxon and Bob Clouse discuss the script while producer Fred Weintraub listens in. The experience in Hollywood filmmaking brought to the project by these men was a significant reason for its success in America.

Surrounded by his most personal guards, the evil Han, played by actor Shih Kien, looks on as his private martial arts tournament proceeds.

called arts, deadly arts that have long been a way of life for a disciplined few and for some even a means of death.

A Film is Born

If *Enter the Dragon* was given life by any single individual it was by its co-producer, Fred Weintraub. When this creative producer came to Warner Bros., the studio put him in a special position: Creative vice-president. He was the principal idea man. As a film innovator, or "Creative VP," Weintraub was responsible for such movies as *Woodstock, Rage* starring George C. Scott, and *Klute* which won Jane Fonda her Oscar.

But, more than anything a top quality martial arts film was the baby he longed to see born. With *Enter the Dragon* Weintraub finally realized a four-year project that he and his co-producer, Paul Heller, saw through from the start. Weintraub and Heller were in charge during every phase of *Enter the Dragon.*

As the first Hollywood filmmaker to see the potential value of the martial arts as a movie subject, Weintraub started by bringing Warner Bros. a series of Chinese boxing films.

"They said flaty 'no.' They didn't feel there was any potential interest in such a subject," he recalled.

Unshaken by the studio's lack of enthusiasm for his proposal, Weintraub himself supervised the writing of a script on the martial art entitled *Kung Fu*. This project was rejected, although television's popular show of the same name was based upon this original script.

Weintraub then joined forces with producer Paul Heller, a veteran with such impressive credits as *David and Lisa* and *Secret Ceremony* which starred Elizabeth Taylor. Together under the banner of Sequoia Pictures, they supervised the scripting of *Enter the Dragon* by Michael Allin.

Weintraub explains his single-minded determination as more than just good business sense. He held a driving belief that the martial arts were the future's greatest source of action entertainment.

"I'd seen all the old Japanese pictures. I thought most were too stylized and much too long. They were great ideas but much too formal and ritualistic. It was only in the last 20 minutes after three hours of preaching and philosophy that the hero would face off against a dozen men and emerge victorious. That was the exciting part—if you were still awake by that time. The hero was always a superman type. I believe in film heroes. I'm tired of the star being a slob."

It was this hero concept combined with the incredibly sophisticated forms of fighting that appealed most to the team of Weintraub and Heller.

Deadly Ballet

"There's an incomparable beauty that's like a deadly kind of ballet to the martial arts. Regardless of the hostility in them, one can't deny the thrill of watching a great fighter go through his paces."

This doesn't discount the fact either that action and violence were entertaining to film audiences, providing they're not too explicitly bloody or morbid.

"It's a violent world; we don't pretend to be trying to reform people through films, and we don't believe film violence contributes to real violence. In any event, it's entertainment, and that's what we are interested in giving people."

Thanks to Weintraub's and Heller's vision and foresight, Warner Bros. was the first company to use Hollywood film technique and quality in a dramatization of the martial arts. Despite the violence, they claimed they would have no objection to their own children seeing *Enter the Dragon*.

While extras look on, Bruce Lee and John Saxon rehearse a fight scene. Saxon's background in martial arts was quite extensive even before deciding to do the film. Here Lee works out the details of a side kick.

"Martial arts in films are here to stay. They may even be destined to become an American institution like the barroom brawl in Westerns.

"It's much more than a trend or fad. We can only see the arts getting bigger and bigger, with the fights becoming more specialized and becoming combined with guns, knives, the whole array of weapons.

The producing team made no pretense about the film having a message, nor did they offer an excuse.

"It's a straightforward story in which you know who's the good guy and who's the villain. There's no moral and no preaching about good and evil, although good wins in the end. We're not a religious picture."

Courage of Their Convictions

Fueled with the enthusiasm of their convictions Weintraub and Heller carefully assembled the principals of their cast and technical crew, arranging for a cooperative effort with Raymond Chow's Concorde Productions of Hong Kong. Aside from the financial savings of shooting the film in the Orient and using Chinese labor and extras, they required authentic Far

Eastern settings, the Chinese know-how and diligence and their technical expertise when it came to the martial arts.

"We were about to play their ball game in their ball park. I wanted the best of both worlds for *Enter the Dragon* so I got lots of expert advisors in the form of local Chinese," said Weintraub.

February, 1972, found Weintraub, Heller, director Robert Clouse, Bruce Lee, John Saxon, Jim Kelly, the 1971 international middleweight karate champion, and beautiful actress Ahna Capri, setting off for Hong Kong to realize their mutually shared vision: to make a film called *Enter the Dragon*.

Problems in Logistics

Upon arrival in Hong Kong to begin shooting, cast and crew were confronted with immediate problems. Disorientation, jet fatigue, not to mention the change of climate and culture affected all adversely.

Visually, Enter the Dragon *was extremely rich. The beautiful Ahna Capri played John Saxon's love interest. Together (above) they discuss his choice of women. The atmosphere of Hong Kong also added much to the film. Saxon (right) rides in a rickshaw through Hong Kong.*

No one had anticipated the enormity of the job they were about to undertake. Probably the biggest obstacle was trying to meld the two different cultures in order to communicate in the making of the film.

"Their ability to construct would put to shame anything American of comparable price," claimed co-producer Heller.

"Everything was hand made. They had no power tools. And since the most abundant commodity they had at their disposal was human labor they put hundreds of men to work handmaking something.

"Every inch of our sets, was elaborately hand-painted even though in some scenes they're hardly seen," he added.

Every object in the film was hand-crafted. Vases, sculptures, were all the result of hundreds of hours of effort and skill. The bars on the jail used in a scene were hand-sanded from square wood blocks. Whereas American technicians would have bought round dowling for bars, the Chinese sanded them round from square originals.

"The way they did the simplest things was fascinating it was so totally different from any way we'd think of approaching a project. We had only five or six American technicians and 500 Chinese to tell what to do. It was an incredible task. Once we understood each other though things got done magnificently," says Heller.

Probably the major obstacle to overcome and one that was never completely surmounted was the dfference in languages. Many words don't translate directly or have a Chinese equivalent, which made interpreters little help in eliminating the communications gap.

Differences in customs and social proprieties also baffled both sides and resulted in lost time. As Heller explained one instance:

"An assistant prop man forgot to bring a prop one morning and he was so ashamed that he disappeared and didn't come back for three days. He'd lost face, which is a very severe disgrace to the Chinese."

Inclement weather, choppy seas and everyone's getting ill at least once all contributed to extending the original schedule in Hong Kong.

Probably the most serious mishap was when Bruce Lee cut his hand in a scene involving a bottle. Because the Chinese don't have harmless sugar bottles for film work a real one was used. Through no one's fault Bruce was incapacitated as a fighter for a week at a time when only fight scenes remained to be filmed. There were scores of other accidents involving extras and minor players. Bob Wall was hurt once, fortunately nothing serious.

Robert Clouse, veteran director of action adventure films, took it all in stride though. He was prepared for the unexpected while making such an action-packed tale. The inherent dangers being tremendous, Clouse claimed they took every precaution in lowering the accident rate, usually high on a martial arts film.

"When they throw those punches, chops and kicks they aren't faking it. It's something like filming a shoot 'em up Western using real bullets and trying to have near misses with each shot.

"Each move had to be with deadly force and intent but with the accuracy to pull back a fraction of an inch short of the target."

While using a cobra in one scene, Bruce Lee was bitten. The cobra had been de-venomized. Some days it would take hours to position 300 extras and explain what they were to do. Often after finishing up a day with explanations about the next day's shooting half the extras wouldn't show up. It was also extremely difficult to enlist female extras for the film, because in Hong Kong actresses were traditionally looked down upon as loose women. Occasional extras who fancied themselves "the next Bruce Lee" would challenge the Oriental star to a fight and needless to say emerged from it with regrets.

Despite Clouse's vast experience with action stars he stood in awe of Bruce Lee's physical prowess and skill. There were several scenes in which the camera had to be speeded up two or three times normal speed in order to capture Bruce's rapid movements on film.

Lee—A Phenomenon

"If we'd shot him at regular speed it would have blurred. Incredible is the only word I can use. He is a phenomenon," said Clouse.

In one scene in which they tow an unruly martial arts competitor behind their Chinese junk in a dinghy, they almost lost the actor in the dinghy to the choppy sea. Just after they finished filming the scene the boat sank and Australian actor Peter Archer was dumped into the rough China Sea.

Another afternoon while filming at sea they accidentally drifted into Red Chinese waters. If they'd been stopped they'd probably have spent months in jail.

Despite *Enter the Dragon*'s escapist fiction plot there were a few really authentic characters in the film. Director Clouse sent assistants out into Hong Kong's backwater dives to recruit actual derelicts, bums and addicts for certain scenes in the film.

For Clouse himself the original aspect of the film was its unique action. He readily admits that the fights were what the audiences came to see. Although, he claimed, that Bruce Lee had a chance to reveal some of his true acting talent in certain quiet scenes.

"I'd been told 'Bruce doesn't need to act, he's an action guy.' Well, he

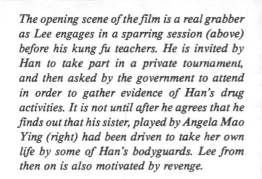

The opening scene of the film is a real grabber as Lee engages in a sparring session (above) before his kung fu teachers. He is invited by Han to take part in a private tournament, and then asked by the government to attend in order to gather evidence of Han's drug activities. It is not until after he agrees that he finds out that his sister, played by Angela Mao Ying (right) had been driven to take her own life by some of Han's bodyguards. Lee from then on is also motivated by revenge.

The spy who stayed out of it all until the last possible minute was Betty Chung, here receiving a stern lecture on the motivation of survival as well as ethical obligations from Bruce Lee.

really surprised me. He's a good actor as well as a supreme martial artist. And vice versa for John Saxon whom we all knew was a fine actor, but who also proved to be a skilled fighter,'' said Clouse.

There is no love interest in the film although there are quite a few lovely young ladies. Purely an adventure film strung together with Bruce Lee's fantastically choreographed fights, *Enter the Dragon* is a film that appeals to the general public and not just a selected few karate experts.

"It's exciting entertainment regardless of how much you know about the martial arts. Of course, the more you know the more you'll notice and appreciate. But a knowledge of the arts is not a prerequisite for enjoying the film,'' said Clouse.

"To me a very dull thing would be a film about a real karate tournament. That would be for the expert. While the action in the film we made is realistic, it's scaled up a bit to the point where it can be enjoyed by most people.''

Clouse hoped *Enter the Dragon* would get the average person interested in the martial arts.

"It's great exercise and discipline. I may take up studying it myself,'' he said.

According to Clouse, shooting the film on location was a priceless asset in achieving the high quality and authenticity demanded for *Enter the Dragon*.

Authentic Locales

"You couldn't recreate that Oriental atmosphere of Hong Kong on a Hollywood sound stage for a million bucks," he exclaimed.

"The sights, sounds, even the smells all combined to create a feeling of intense realism for the people involved in the production. I believe that realistic quality comes across on screen.

"Hong Kong is truly the teeming city of the Far East. The small sampans rowing in and out of the harbor anytime of day or night, the hustle and bustle or a rural trade center as people make their way about carrying bundles, the weathered and wise faces of the old people who have seen so much; it's all a part of this intriguing city."

Although the island of Han is only a figment of a skilled photographer's imagination in creating a composite picture from three entirely different locales, director Clouse had no doubt that there are really several actual islands of Han in existence.

"I wouldn't be surprised at anything about the Orient. It holds endless mysteries and possibilities. It's truly one of the last bastions of intrigue left on earth."

Kurt Hirshler, editor of *Enter the Dragon* and veteran of such films as *The Fugitive Kind* starring Marlon Brando, *Splendor in the Grass,* and *They Came to Cordura,* is the man responsible for distilling the massive footage of film shot on location into a coherent, cohesive story.

"Although in many respects an action film is an action film when it comes to editing, I got a genuine education working with footage of Bruce Lee. He's so lightning fast yet everything he does is perfect," he said.

As editor, Hirshler had the opportunity to scrutinize Lee's style in a situation in which he could stop the film, slow it down or run it faster than normal.

"There aren't even signals he gives—not a hint that he's going to throw a punch. He's also in possession of incredible energy. He'd often have to do 10-15 takes of one fight scene, and he'd rarely show any fatigue. I got tired just watching him on film as I edited it!"

Hirshler claimed that because of the physical expertise of the martial artists involved in the picture, particularly Lee, none of the action was faked nor was it made to look more proficient than it actually was through editing room tricks. All of the feats performed were actually done and at the speed shown, except for a couple of slow-motion sequences in which the real speed was of course, faster.

"There are many long takes in which I was told not to cut in and out with close-ups because the karate routines were so perfect. The camera ran as the martial artists did their routines, and I left it in the film as such. It was so perfect it would have been a crime to have tampered with it."

Additional editing time was required however to add the dubbed soundtrack because the Chinese do not shoot sound films. They shoot the visual first and then retreat to the recording studio and add the dialogue later in synchronization to the lip movements.

Ideal Editing Situation

Contrary to general practice, Hirshler went with the film unit to location and observed the shooting so that on return to Hollywood to edit he would have a clear, first-hand idea of what he wanted to do with the film.

"It was the ideal situation for an editor. It was additionally advantageous because I could advise them from week to week during the shooting about certain shots they might need to fill in the story here and there."

Hirshler claimed that he soon picked up what are known as the

Lee's cinematic showdown with Bob Wall was another highlight of the film. Knowing he cannot win by fair means, Wall's character comes at Lee with a broken bottle. Lee blocks his stab with a kick to the wrist.

During Bruce's showdown with Bob Wall, Lee's attempted kick is blocked and Wall traps his leg. Lee shows off his gymnastic talents by doing this spectacular summersault. With his free leg, Lee lands a kick to the chin.

"rhythms" inherent in a martial arts film and cut according to those rhythms. Commonly known, in a sense, as "pace," each type of film has a different ryhthm. A detective film, a war movie, a love story, all have widely varied rhythms that almost unconsciously set the mood of each film. Hirshler explained of *Enter the Dragon*.

"You must allow yourself to be open and receptive to whatever material you're editing. You must allow the film to dictate how to cut it. *Dragon* had very definite rhythms and was an extremely upbeat and fast-paced film.

"Editing is not dissimilar to sculpting, in which there is a concept that the sculptor, whether he be working with marble, clay or film, must liberate and reveal the figure inherent in the material. Almost as if the figure and form are in there and its the sculptor's or editor's job to help that form be born."

With the addition of Lalo Schifrin's superb musical score, *Enter the Dragon* had become a complete reality. It had been born and had a life of its own.

Perhaps co-producer Paul Heller summed it up best in his observation that the secret to *Enter the Dragon*'s success was in its fundamental assertion of the individual as a hero.

"A guy who goes to see this film can once again feel that maybe he too can change his life for the better: right wrongs, improve things for everyone. Despite the violence in the film, there is the net positive good.

"The lone hero is a great and traditional kind of story that's particularly American. And even though *Enter the Dragon* was of an Oriental subject, its basic theme was thoroughly American in attitude."

Add that to the genuine curiosity that Americans have always had for the mysteries of the Orient, most of which have yet to unfold for the West and you could not help but have a winning combination.

PART 4

Chapter 10

Bruce Lee as Seen Through the Eyes of Movie Personalities

STEVE McQUEEN

I met Bruce in Los Angeles in 1968 or 69. I'm not involved in the martial arts to any degree. I'm not an expert or anything like that. Bruce was just a personal friend of mine, and I cared for him a lot. Sometimes I'd feel rotten and the phone would ring, and it would be Bruce. I don't know why he called. He would just say, "I just thought I should call you."

I thought Bruce was a brilliant, fine philosopher about everyday living, and I was very taken with his theories and approach to the martial arts. He was very much into finding out who he was. His comment to people was, "Know yourself." Know yourself, I would imagine, through the martial arts, which was some type of extension of himself. But he also knew himself in everyday life. The good head that he acquired was through his knowing himself. He and I used to have great long discussions about that. No matter what you do in life, you don't know yourself, you're never going to be able to appreciate anything in life. That, I think, is today's mark of a good human being—to know yourself.

I thought a great deal of Bruce. He was a wonderful guy.

JAMES COBURN

I met Bruce through Stirling Silliphant. Bruce came over and brought a couple of pieces of apparatus with him—an inflatable tube or football thing that he used to kick with, and an inflatable bladder that he held up. When he asked me what I knew about martial arts, I told him. "Very little; only what I've done in the *Flint* series."

Bruce said his technique was really no technique because it was *all* the techniques, and only the individual could accomplish them. He said, "I can give you the tools, but you have to develop your own way of using them. Here, I'll show you. From one inch I can deliver a very powerful punch." He handed me a pillow and knocked me down in the back of a chair. I rolled all the way over to the sofa. I just went *Bang! Blast! Whap!* It was really funny.

I said, "Let's go to work!" and we started working together. I wanted to see how much I could do. I was trying to find the most efficient method of studying a martial art. The other forms seemed to involve so much of a ritual, so much attention to school and type . . . the kind of achievements that you wear around your waist. It seemed too militaristic and it didn't really appeal to me. That's why I hadn't done anything since *Flint*.

So Bruce and I worked out. He showed me how to hit. In one lesson he taught me how to punch, which is very simple. It's taking everything to its logical extremity, making the energy totally usable—no tense energy—where everything goes *Pow!* right there. It's like a hose, like the end of a whip. That's where all of the energy eventually goes.

Bruce taught me side kicks and hook kicks. He got me breaking two-inch boards with my side kick, holding them by two fingers, which I felt was really an accomplishment. For me, it was. For him, it was nothing. He could break three of them. He'd toss them up in the air and kick them.

But Bruce didn't teach. He allowed *you* to. He would place you in a circumstance where you could evolve yourself. He would say, "Not that, not that, not that!" and you would know. He would just look at you, and *Bam!* "Okay, again!" until you could feel what was the optimum. Then you could expand from there. He would show you style, the style for you, and try to get your body to move in those things. We'd do specific exercises that my body needed, and then we designed a series of exercises I could continue when I was on location—so I could work out by myself.

There was great concentration and focus of attention when we were working, which is something that I really like. When I am working on something, it's great to have somebody else working on the same thing so that you have all of that energy. It doubles the energy and your focus of attention becomes something else. Then it's no longer work. It's an involvement of the moment.

Bruce shows his gentler side as he listens attentively in Fists of Fury.

Bruce taught through impressions. He would lay down an aphorism, a Chinese saying, or a saying that he would have made up out of a combination of Oriental and Western thought, in a way that was applicable to the moment but that could spread out and be applicable universally. I believe that the martial arts are limited and you can only extend them so far, and I believe this is what Bruce found—that there is an absolute limit that you can reach.

We worked together for about two-and-a-half years. When I wasn't working, we worked out every other day, about three days a week. I sometimes went to his place, where there was a lot of apparatus to use. We'd work out for an hour, then we'd talk for an hour about a lot of things. Bruce always related everything to the martial arts, or the martial arts to everything. He didn't separate life from the extension in his arm. And he is the only one I know of that carried it to the point of real art. I imagine in the old days when the martial arts were created there were a lot of artists. But Bruce was the only "martial *artist*" I know of. He had great enthusiasm.

Bruce once injured his back when he was doing a television show. From what the doctor said, he had too much muscle around his rib cage. He did a high kick, and the tension broke two of his ribs and pulled a muscle in his back. Finally, the muscle spasm got so bad that it laid him down for about three months. He had to give up teaching. In this short time, he wrote something like three books of his thoughts, and ideas, and synthesized technique.

Bruce was an avid reader and had a great library—both in Chinese and English—about the martial arts and weapons of all kinds. He knew how to use them all. Any man that can lay down and not die for three months from total inactivity, and transfer his obsession into three or four volumes of writings, is an artist.

There was no one, real Bruce Lee. There were a lot of them. I saw a change take place. He was moving on a 45-degree angle, climbing all the time—*all* the time—no matter what was happening. He was always changing. He was always facing new problems, new things. Finally, at the end, I think certain things overwhelmed him.

The last time I saw him, which was just before his death, he was just beginning to settle in the atmosphere of fame, which is a hard one to get used to. It causes you to do a lot of things that you wished you hadn't done. And I think Bruce was feeling this in his ego because of the great acclaim that he got. He had no doubt.

The first time I saw him, I had no doubt that he was the greatest martial artist that I had ever witnessed; probably one of the greatest of all time. And he knew it, too. I mean it wasn't a question of him competing with anybody.

Bruce's ability to concentrate his energy was one of the attributes most noted by friends such as James Coburn who saw this talent not only as a reason for his success as a martial artist but as the potential of his further development as an actor.

It was a question of everbody else competing with *him* because he was like the beacon, the source of the energy that everybody got something from.

So the thing that plugged Bruce up, the bogged him down, was success. And it was something that he had always wanted more than anything else: the success of achieving something with martial arts without making any compromises anywhere down the line—absolutely none. But finding, at the end, that there *is* a limit and that your technique has evolved to that high degree, then humanity must be the next step. Bruce was like an arrow, with a single pointed *sshhhot,* a great energy, hitting the mark and exploding. He hit the mark!

Bruce was brilliant in *Enter the Dragon*. But I don't think he would ever have attempted anything other than a martial art part. He couldn't because he couldn't act, and I berated him constantly for this when I saw him over there (in Hong Kong). But he said that it wasn't necessary for the Southwest Chinese. They think it's great. And it is! That's his tradition, you see. But I think it was his lack, really, for not being open enough to allow someone to show him what "character" was, how to play, how to do those things. Bruce caricatured everything. It was like the Chinese tradition of acting with heavy masks and with very defined, rigid characters. And he played the mask, rather than the emotional. Had he learned to act, it probably wouldn't have made any difference at all at the box office. But I think it would have made more difference overall. I think it would have been a legacy of total artistry.

But Bruce was the Nijinsky of martial arts. He could *do* it. He could do all that stuff that was on film, whereas, with the other guys, everything is done in quick cuts and a lot of movie tricks. Bruce really did them. To watch him work was amazing. He was incredibly inventive when it came to fights. The problem with the fights, from my point of view, was he was always dominant. There was a lack of vulnerability. He was like a superman, which works on a certain level, but he should have dealt with higher things if he was a superman. He should have dealt with higher principles.

JOHN SAXON

Bruce was very, very helpful to me. My main interest with him was in questioning him about the martial arts, and we were constantly talking about that sort of thing. He was helpful in showing me a lot of things that I think were probably part of his teaching that people paid a lot of dough to learn.

As a martial artist—which is what Bruce considered himself first and foremost—he was very innovative. He was able to see the potential weaknesses and defects of any particular system. Therefore, he joined many things together, which I think was very important. His basic idea was that fighting, as such, is a very fluid and non-systematic kind of thing. Moreover, he was able to personally utilize this kind of investigation in the martial arts and really become something very creative and self-expressive in the process; I mean, not only from the standpoint of films, which, of course, we know he eventually got into and became immensely successful at, but strictly in the business of the art itself. He was able to express himself, his beliefs and ideas, his concepts of reality, and he tested that reality. I would agree that he was a genius, or certainly near genius, with regard to the martial arts.

As an actor, I would say Bruce had a great deal of theater—theatricality. In certain respects, I think he wasn't anywhere near the actor that he was the martial artist. But he had a very strong savvy about theater and how to present himself, which in effect, with all his talent, was theatricality. He was very, very clever and was really acting as an actor and, in a sense, a director and a writer because he was writing scripts in his genre. He told me a couple of plot lines that he had. The way he presented himself in films was, in a sense, a very theatrical idea, one of which, as an actor, I admired.

I think the ultimate question was one that could have been a potential problem with someone like Bruce had he continued his career. I said to him, "Would you now want to play parts that have nothing to do with the martial arts," even parts where he would have to surrender or belie his great physical ability? And he said, yeah, he kind of considered that kind of thing. That would have been the test that he would have had to face one day, if he'd wanted to do that. It's a very difficult thing. Immediately, the public begins to identify you with one thing, and it sometimes becomes very difficult for them to believe you doing another thing.

Bruce was extremely buoyant. He was really enjoying many parts of the success which he was having, which was a pleasure to watch. He really related to the people in Hong Kong who loved him. They really reacted to him, and he enjoyed them. He enjoyed kibitzing with the cab drivers, with

Bruce and John Saxon became very good friends as a result of Enter the Dragon.

the kids from the age of five or so who recognized and adulated him. It was a pleasure to watch, rather than some people with public positions who don't like to mingle and who say, "Get them off my back!" or "I don't want to be bothered!" I mean, it was really a problem, but Bruce enjoyed it to the point where it wasn't a problem anymore.

Bruce was a very intelligent guy—very intelligent. The few lengthy conversations that I had with him, he displayed a great deal of native intelligence and savvy in many things. I think one of the things Bruce talked about that was very important was just the getting away from any kind of static image of yourself when doing what you're doing; in other words, the reality of it, rather than the theatricality. Theatricality is okay for movies, but the reality of—let's say, fighting—is something that is very spontaneous, and Bruce emphasized it. You had to be as good as he was, or near it anyway, before you could appreciate that most people have to learn to do this by imitation, by repetition, almost by rote. Bruce had a great deal of spontaneity, which is very important in all things: acting, life, whatever; certainly in fighting, and I'm no great judge of that.

Personally, Bruce and I got along very well. There was some sort of mutual appreciation. I think he liked me, and I liked him very much. It's a great pity that at this peak of his career something went wrong and he died.

JIM KELLY

I first heard about Bruce when he was doing the TV show *The Green Hornet.* Everybody was talking about it. "Yeah, the Green Hornet. He's bad, he's bad." And I said, "Hey, cm'on! I have got to see this program." But I never did get a chance to see it.

Before I met Bruce, though, I had read material on him—different articles in BLACK BELT magazine—and I had heard a lot of people talk about him; how good he was. "Bruce Lee this, and Bruce Lee that." I said, "Doggone! If this guy is half as bad as these people are talking about, he's got to be bad!" I saw Bruce in a movie called *Marlowe,* and he impressed me quite a bit there. He was very cool. So I already had this idea, this image of Bruce, before I met him.

And then when I met Bruce, there was just something about him. He called me when I arrived in Hong Kong to film *Enter the Dragon*. Here he is— Bruce Lee, superstar. I thought, "This is a real gentleman, a real man. This guy has really got it put together." We went out to dinner and we talked about different things. I developed a thing where I could listen to him talk all day, all night. He talked about himself a lot. But he had a lot to say. It was like listening to Muhammad Ali talk; same thing. So I enjoyed listening to Bruce.

Bruce was the type of person that had to be moving all the time, doing things all the time—really involved in doing something. He couldn't sit still. He was not that type of person. He had to talk, even about himself, and I could dig it because he was a very interesting person . . . everything he talked about was heavy.

To me, Bruce Lee was like Muhammad Ali. He was that type of character. There was an article on Muhammad Ali that I showed to Bruce once, and he just sat there and read and read and read. And that time when George Foreman was in that Joe Frazier fight, we were on the set, and the guys were putting makeup on, and Bruce just kept reading about the fight. He was the type of guy that, when he sees something good, he just looks at it, keeps studying it, trying to create something in his own image. I really dig it!

Then when I worked out with Bruce, he showed me some techniques. We worked on different sparring techniques and stuff. Damn! This guy is heavy —very heavy guy. His techniques were so dynamic, man, and he was so powerful for his size, so powerful. One time he said, "Jim, throw your backhand." So I threw my backhand a couple of times. Then he said, "You have a pretty fast backhand, you know. Let me throw mine at you." So I got ready, Bruce threw his backhand and I blocked it. He said. "You blocked my backhand! Man, *nobody* blocks my backhand!" Jokingly, you know. He wasn't serious. He was just kidding.

So little things like this added up to other things, and I got to know Bruce. I developed the utmost respect for him. Just from the short time I was in Hong Kong, we became very close—more like a brotherly thing.

During rehearsals for *Enter the Dragon*, Bruce gave me respect as a martial artist to do whatever I wanted to do. He didn't say, "Jim, this is what you are going to do. That's it!" Before we even got into the fight scenes, which he choreographed, he said, "Jim, I want you to do what you want to do. I know that you did your technical advising on *Melinda*. You know your art, and you can do whatever you want to do." So I did the fight scene in the stadium myself. Bruce had something laid out, and he said, "Jim, do you

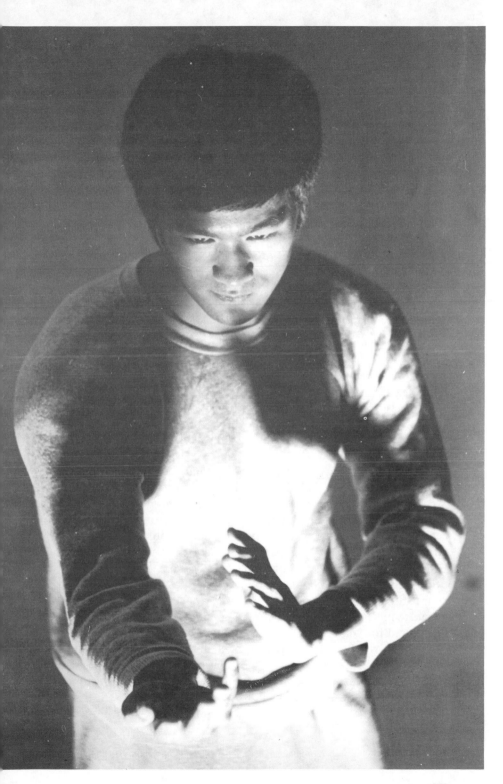

Bruce takes on a karate expert in Way of the Dragon. *Though his roots were in kung fu, Bruce studied and liked to feature many styles in his films.*

like this?'' I said, ''I may change this and that.'' But it wasn't, ''Hey, Jim! This is it. You got to do it cause I'm Bruce Lee. I'm the technical adviser.'' It wasn't that type of thing, so I was able to change quite a few things around in that particular fight to the way I felt comfortable doing it.

We were doing an interview one time on the set and the guy wanted to interview me, but he couldn't speak English. So Bruce was the interpreter. He asked Bruce, ''Bruce, ask Jim what he thinks of Bruce Lee,'' I said, ''Hey, Bruce, you tell him that Bruce Lee talks a lot of B.S. But he can back up his B.S.'' Bruce was very comical, very funny, but I was very serious.

Several times Bruce and I just went to the side and talked. We just rapped . . . very serious. And I told him, ''Bruce, I have the utmost respect for you because of what you have done for yourself personally, your personal achievement in life, and what you have done for your people—the type of image you have set for your people, giving them someone to look up to. Especially in this type of environment, they need someone to look up to, and I think it's great what you have done for your people and family, and just your entire accomplishment in life.'' I was very serious and he knew it, and he said to me, ''Jim, you know what? I hope you do the same thing for your people and for yourself.''

I think it was harder for Bruce to break into show business than for me because when Bruce was doing his thing, he was the one who had to pave the way. He's Chinese, and I don't know any Chinese superstar actors in the United States. So Bruce was the number-one man. Bruce was the first one to do this. I have people who are before me: Jim Brown, Sidney Poitier, some other black actors. They laid the path; they opened up the doors. Bruce didn't have anyone to open up the doors for him as far as his nationality was concerned, but I did. It's still not easy for me now, but it's easier than what it was for Bruce. He was the first one to lay the foot down in the States, as far as Oriental actors are concerned. So I feel that it did help Bruce a lot to go back to the Orient and establish himself and then come on the way he did.

If Bruce had lived, he would have no doubt been a superstar here. He still is. People who never knew him personally had a lot of respect for him; a *lot* of people, especially black people. "Bruce Lee is my idol." They see two movies of Bruce Lee and this guy is their idol. So there is no doubt he would have been making a million dollars a picture.

A guy who owns a karate studio came by my studio once and said, "Hey, Jim how good is Bruce Lee?" And I said, "Hey, man, you're in the karate business. You're supposed to have knowledge in karate. You can *see* how good he is." He said, "Well, a lot of people I know say he isn't any good. He's just good on the screen." So some people are really jealous, envious. First, you have to have a strong mind like Bruce had to forget about these people. They are only mentioning this to tear you down. But as far as commercial schools—all karate schools—are concerned, I'm sure they are glad for Bruce, glad for the martial arts movies, because this gives them more business. Every time a new movie comes out, their enrollment jumps up.

Bruce and I were very similar in one sense. We found out that we wanted to do, and we did it. I have different ideals about karate and which way I like to do my techniques that are different from the regular karate system; I mean, way of blocking, way of punching, way of dancing, way you use your footwork. I thought up all these things when I got my black belt, and I started really analyzing what's happening. I said, "Well, I am going to study Muhammad Ali's boxing field, watch his footwork, use his footwork, study his movements, and study wrestlers and judomen and all these different types of arts and then combine them together into my own thing." I said, "Maybe I'm crazy to do this because nobody else does this." But I found that Bruce did the same thing.

So we sat down and talked for two or three hours. I thought of all these things, and Bruce thought of all these things on the same level. So I could understand. We really understood each other on this level; the way he thought, the way I think. It's like you can do anything you want to do and nobody can stop you. All you have to do is set that goal and find the necessary steps it takes to reach that goal. And you can do it, no matter if you're black, white, Oriental, or whatever it may be. That's what Bruce thought, and that's the way I think.

Chapter 11

Bruce Lee as Seen Through the Eyes of Movie Executives

STIRLING SILLIPHANT

I met Bruce about five or six years ago. I had heard stories about his tremendous speed and ability, and I had seen him on *The Green Hornet*, in which he played Kato. For some time, I had been wanting to get involved in martial arts. But I was searching for a freer style than I felt, at that time, karate could afford me. I wanted something more adaptable to streetfighting. And I just couldn't find anyone who seemed to understand what I was looking for in terms of personal exercise and getting my body and head together.

One of my major interests for the last 15 years has been a study of Oriental philosophies, particularly of Zen. I felt that the martial arts were an extension of these disciplines. So I went looking for Bruce. It took me about six months to find someone who could introduce me to him, but at last he came to my offices at Columbia Pictures. I told him I wanted to study with him.

Bruce said, "I think you're too old. I don't believe there's a chance your reflexes are good enough to do what I'd want you to do." So I did a few

Producer/writer Stirling Silliphant and Bruce Lee spent many hours together discussing and developing ideas for film scripts.

things, and he seemed pleased and surprised. He said okay, he'd take me on as a student.

Joe Hyams, the writer, and I took lessons together two or three times a week from Bruce for a year. I got so interested I preferred to study alone with Bruce, which I did for another year, three times a week, advancing to what he called his second stage. When I got to that stage, he had me running three miles every morning and working out, and I was in absolutely beautiful condition.

During this time, in any of the films I was writing, I always tried either to incorporate Bruce as an actor or as a behind-the-scenes stuntman whenever I could. For example, I wrote a film at MGM called *Marlowe* with James Garner. I put two sequences into it—the two best scenes in the film—where Bruce comes into Garner's office and tears it up and another when he meets Garner up on the roof of the Occidental building and goes kicking and screaming off into space. That probably was Bruce's first American feature film appearance.

Bruce was such a dear friend, and I had such tremendous respect for his absolutely God-given talent, that whenever I could put him into anything I would just make up things to get him into the film. The next project I did was a film for Columbia called *A Walk in the Spring Rain*; a love story. I wrote a fight scene into it which took place in the Tennessee mountains. Since the story was located in the South, I couldn't write any Orientals into the fight because they simply don't have Asians down there in Gatlinburg. But I did bring Bruce down to Tennessee to choreograph and stage the fight.

There were a couple of stuntmen—big, tough Caucasian cats—assigned to the movie who were very skeptical about Bruce. They saw this 135-pound Chinese who, when he didn't want to look tough, could maintain a very low profile. Bruce and I were hanging around together, and they kind of resented the fact that an outside guy—not a member of the stuntmen's union—was in charge of them. I made it very clear to them, since I was not only the writer but the producer, that Bruce was the boss on their fight sequence and they'd damn well follow his orders. But they kept putting him on and he was getting very uptight, so I said, "Listen, why don't you just give them a little sample of what a side kick can do?"

Bruce had brought down the air shield because he and I were working out all the time. He had me practicing my spin kicks and jumping kicks on the shield. So he said to them, "One of you guys hold this shield. I'm going to give it a little kick. But I suggest you brace yourself first. I kick pretty hard." And they said, "Oh, sure, sure." And I said, "Hey, Bruce, to make it interesting, let's do it out by the swimming pool." So Bruce told the first guy to brace himself. With no movement at all—no run, no nothing, just standing there in front of him—Bruce kicked this guy, lifted him off his feet, up into the air, and out into the pool! Well, that guy came up a Christian! From that moment on, he would have killed for Bruce.

Now the other guy hadn't gotten religion yet. He figured the other stuntman was pure chicken. So he really got down low, like a football lineman—all six-feet-two, 190 pounds of muscle—and braced himself. Bruce knocked him right off his feet and into the water. And I don't mean with any preparation; just like that, just like you're standing talking and suddenly, like a backhand takeoff. . . . So, from that moment on, these guys loved Bruce.

Then I was doing a television show called *Longstreet*. I had sold the series with a 90-minute pilot film. Now the time had come to do the first, on-the-air one-hour episode. Together, Bruce and I worked out our opening story. I called it "The Way of the Intercepting Fist," which was, of course, the literal translation of "jeet kune do," Bruce's personal martial art. It was a very straightline story in which James Franciscus, the blind detective, is assaulted by some toughs in the beginning and told to keep off the dock. He is saved from being hurt by a Chinese antique dealer—Bruce—who just happens to be walking by and clobbers these guys with kicks and punches.

The detective wants to get back at his assailants and asks Bruce what he did and how he did it. But Bruce doesn't want to teach him because the blind man's motivation for learning is wrong. So the story had to do with teaching Franciscus how to learn the way of the intercepting fist.

We had more fan mail on that episode than on any of the other shows we did in the series. Bruce, in turn, got a tremendous volume of letters and reactions from both critics and viewers. As a matter of fact, it was that episode which gave him, I like to believe, his first good film to show himself off to the world with pride and dignity as an Oriental martial artist. And even though I wrote it, I think it probably was the best martial art film that has ever been on the air. What I did was simply to take many of the things Bruce had taught me and put them into the script. In any event, as a result of that episode, the network (ABC) and Paramount wanted Bruce in more episodes. Ultimately we used him in three other *Longstreet*s during that year before he went to Hong Kong and rose to superstar status. It was after this first TV episode he was approached by Ted Ashley of Warner Bros. and by Screen Gems (as well as by Paramount) to sign for a series they hoped to develop for him.

Longstreet was the last thing Bruce did in America in terms of films until he went to Hong Kong and did the other films, and then I lost close track of him, although I did see him in Hong Kong while I was there doing research on another film. He met me at the airport and took me to dinner. It was such an incredible thing to watch the difference in his life-style—between the

Bruce's natural intensity helped him to immediately achieve the kind of powerful screen presence that took other actors years of training to project.

U.S. and Hong Kong—because here in the States he was always fighting the battle of any minority person has to fight. I can tell you it's almost impossible for an Asian actress or actor to get much of a part in American films. This was the thing that Asian actors battled constantly with little success. Bruce did beat it. When he was here, he never compromised his dignity. As he said, he would never take a part as a pigtailed coolie. He would never play a "heathen Chinese." He was always Bruce Lee.

It was incredible that Bruce always knew he would someday be the most important star in the world. I had serious doubts he would ever achieve what he ultimately achieved. In terms of his being one of the great martial artists of all time, I didn't have any doubts. And I knew he had tremendous magnetism on the screen. When I saw his first two Chinese-made films in Hong Kong, I was absolutely delighted to see that same force and energy, which he projected here on our TV series, come out even more there. But to predict that he would have the success that he did around the world . . . it was like a dream that couldn't come true. It was like saying that the Oriental minority is no longer a minority but has been accepted. Bruce was more than just a single success story. He represented a whole race finally being accepted in films.

There is so much emotion on my part in terms of what Bruce meant to me. It wasn't just the fact that he taught me martial arts. It was the fact that he was the first person who ever taught me to see one of the underlying reasons why I studied martial arts in the beginning—that my relationships with men had never been the way a lot of other men's relationships seem to be naturally. I am a writer. I am essentially a very private person. I never hung out with the boys. Unlike a lot of guys who go out bowling on Thursday nights with the guys, I never had any men friends. All of my friends were women. You begin to wonder. You say to yourself, "Hey, I wonder if maybe something's the matter with me. Why am I not like the other guys?"

I never cared too much for football. Baseball puts me to sleep. I always went in for individual sports. I was on the fencing team at USC for three years. But that's man-to-man. And that's why I loved martial arts. It was me against the other guy. I never liked team stuff, and Bruce made all that come clear—about what all that means.

Bruce was the first man I ever put my arm around. We are taught in this country that if you touch a guy maybe you're a fag, so we are always kind of reluctant to have physical contact with men—except in sports.

When I tell you that I loved this man, it was because he made me realize that you should look at all human beings not in a sexual sense but in a human sense. They aren't just men and women; they are people. Bruce cleared up in my head, for all time, the confusion about that. Now I can take a guy's hand if I feel like it and hold it, and if someone calls me a fag, I laugh at them. I don't even get hostile because it's no challenge; it's no threat.

Bruce taught me so many things without teaching me. He was a very remarkable human being. He may be the only person I ever met in my whole life, and may ever meet, who was truly a master of what he did. It's kind of impossible to meet guys like that. Well, I guess I do know others. I have tremendous respect, affection, and love for Tak Kubota, who, in shotokan karate, is an absolute perfect master. Jhoon Rhee, whom I know and am very fond of, is a master of tae kwon do. These are also great, great men in terms of their total dedication, their simplicity.

Bruce was very pure. He was only one thing. He was a master. He was, in a sense, almost inhuman in his ability. He never stopped his dedication or his training. James Coburn and I went to India with him on a research and reconnaissance trip. All the time we were there, Bruce would be kicking, or stretching, or punching, or moving. He was like a cat. But when he was still, he was still. He was always aware of his body and of his art, and that's all he lived for. He was the most dedicated man I've ever known in my life.

FRED WEINTRAUB

I go back about three or four years with Bruce. I am not interested in practicing the martial arts. I mean, I'm not a physical kind of guy at all. But I had the feeling there was going to be a resurgence of what I call the "super-hero" movies. In fact, I had a script written some time ago called *Kung Fu*, which eventually became the television show. I have always loved Chinese pictures. Technically, I hate them because they take three hours before the final shoot-out. But in the end, it is one guy against 200. It's always great!

We decided to do *Enter the Dragon* before any of his Chinese pictures opened in America. I had had a script written for Bruce. It was a Western called *Kelsey,* which was never done, but I thought Bruce would have been fantastic in the part. I had seen *The Big Boss* (released in the United States as

In what has since become a famous Bruce Lee pose, Bruce holds up the nunchaku. Until he made it popular, the nunchaku was a little-known weapon to the general public. Bruce's flair inspired many more to begin learning it. Unlike those who would follow, however, Bruce used nunchaku sticks connected by a fairly long rope or chain. Nunchaku with longer ropes or chains are more difficult to control and more dangerous for the user.

Fists of Fury) and I thought he was sensational in it. So I went to Hong Kong to see him and met Raymond Chow. We put together a deal which we were going to do with their company (Golden Harvest, Ltd.) in mind. Then after I came back, Warner Bros. got interested and decided to become a partner.

Bruce had something you can't define. How can you define charisma? He had something on screen where you couldn't keep your eyes off him. There's no question about that. His tremendous intensity—something I have rarely seen in films—comes across on the screen. Some people have it and it doesn't come across. But Bruce had it, and there was no question! You were with him all the way.

Enter the Dragon was the first time Bruce had ever worked with a good director like Robert Clouse, and I think the combination of the two of them was really good. They worked together. Bruce choreographed the fights, and the director told him what angles would make it work. I think that's very important. It's one thing to choreograph a fight; it's another thing to get the fight so that it looks right. Nobody got killed. Those punches are not all hits. On occasion, they are, but 99 percent of the time they are not.

Bruce did hurt himself during the filming. There is a fight scene where Bob Wall holds some bottles, and Bruce cut his hands because we had no breakaway glass in Hong Kong. Bruce was a great exponent of his own body, and I think he was terribly upset that anything hurt his body. I knew him well. He wouldn't even let me smoke in his presence. He was a great guardian of his own physical well-being. He was the most protective guy for his own physical well-being I ever met.

There were many funny incidents between the Americans and the Chinese who were working on the film. We had great difficulties in language. We'd ask for birds and we got frogs! But we were the first who have ever been able to shoot with a complete Chinese crew and only three Americans.

I think it was a combination of things that earned Bruce the status he achieved. One was his tremendous interest in his own physical thing and his knowledge of martial arts. I was out with Bruce one day when we were with California Senator John Tunney. The senator was very interested in Bruce and asked him, "By the way, did you know my father (former world heavyweight boxing champion Gene Tunney)?" and Bruce replied, "Not only did I know your father, but I've read all of his books." This was the first time John Tunney had known anybody in the world who had read his father's books. I mean, Bruce was so well-versed and knowledgeable about fighting styles, and he was a great reader. He was not a gregarious guy who had many friends. In a funny kind of way, he was shy, and he spent many hours alone reading. Yet, put him on stage or with the crew, and he was very gregarious.

Had Bruce lived, I think he would have become another hero like Douglas Fairbanks, Jr., Errol Flynn, or Clint Eastwood. He would have become the superaction superstar. I mean, nobody would have competed with him. And nobody will ever replace him. You don't replace people in the motion picture business. There will be someone else. Somewhere in America, there's a kid right now about 12 years old who is seeing Bruce Lee's films and is saying, "I'm going to do that!" He's starting to work right now, and in about eight or ten years there he will be! Somebody always comes along with a different style, a different idea, a different method of functioning. There was John Wayne, and now there's Clint Eastwood, and that's the way it works. But you don't "replace" somebody like Bruce Lee."

Chapter 12

Bruce Lee as Seen Through the Eyes of TV Personalities

VAN WILLIAMS

Bruce was far progressed in the martial arts at the time I met him. It was a religion to him . . . his whole way of life. Acting was a very secondary thing. Of anybody I have ever known that stuck with one thing, well, that was Bruce Lee. He perfected it to the point where he was head-and-shoulders above everybody else. Once his star started rising in Asia, he got very busy. I am sure that he perfected it even more.

Bruce's style and flair were primarily something designed for him. It was his idea and his interpretation of what these things should be, and his background as a dancer gave him a tremendous amount of spring in his legs—plus he was extremely fast. I have never known anybody that worked so hard to physically develop himself; not with weights, but strenghtening his muscles with dynamic tension and all that stuff that he did. I went to see a number of championship karate tournaments with Bruce when he was doing an exhibition. He was so far ahead of everybody else, it was like there was one man, and everybody else in that profession looked up to that one man. This is the way it was done. If you were going to build yourself up anyway, you did it the way Bruce Lee did it.

I felt Bruce was kind of in the wrong place there in *The Green Hornet*. The stuff that he did in the series was probably the most popular part of the show—the action sequences doing his kung fu and the fight scenes we did. He got quite a following out of that—a worldwide following. I felt it was just a matter of time. That's the irony of the thing. It is still one of the gripes I've got about the business as it is nowadays: you still have to go abroad to become a star. Nobody could really see what this guy had to offer as far as worldwide popularity is concerned. He had to go abroad, but the Asians finally saw what he had—primarily, I think, through *The Green Hornet* series because it ran in Japan and, as far as I know, in Hong Kong as well as other places.

I've never known a much finer person in my life than Bruce. He was a very good friend. I could rely on him for just about anything that I ever asked him, and vice versa.

Bruce seemed to get along with everybody; everybody seemed to get along with him. About the only thing I could say that detracted from him was his rather short fuse; not between the two of us; but he did have a short fuse every now and then as far as his personality was concerned. He could

Bruce's martial arts techniques, such as this side kick, were as much driven by his inner passion for transcendence as by the muscles of his body.

Even in candid shots Bruce was very photogenic. His features were expressive. Many thought he did not fully realize his potential as an actor.

take just so much stuff if it was a putdown to him or to his profession. I really considered his profession to be the martial arts—not acting. If he would have worked on the acting business as much as he did the martial arts, he would have been a huge star that way, too.

Bruce was a fine, fine man and did not let that business go to his head. He always kept his head on his shoulders. He enjoyed it. I've never known anybody that enjoyed it or wanted success and fame that way more than he did, and he stuck with it and got it!

Bruce had a great sense of humor and was always kidding around and telling jokes. He had a great memory for jokes. It was always kind of a light thing. We had a big problem with that show as in a lot of the shows they do now. Before we even got started, we were a day behind. And everybody was panic-city from the time we got started until the time we finished a show, which should have been three or four days later, but which was usually four or five. It took an awful lot of hard work to get that show done, and we worked some long hours on it. All of a sudden, the tension would build up, and then Bruce would pop out with one of his jokes, and it would kind of relax everybody.

It's a pitiful thing to see a guy 32 years old starting off in a fantastic career. . . . He was just starting to break open that whole thing—worldwide—even more so than James Dean because Bruce had a talent. Dean was an actor, but Bruce Lee had an aura around him, being the top man in the martial arts business (if that's what you want to call it) throughout the world. I feel like I have lost a very dear friend. I miss the guy.

JAMES FRANCISCUS

I didn't know Bruce much more than working with him that month and a half on *Longstreet*, but I considered him to be a friend, and we got along very well. He helped me a lot on the set. We had a show where the martial arts were used in one whole act against a fellow, and Bruce brought me through all of that and taught me enough basics so it looked like I knew what I was doing. I really didn't, but. . . .

Bruce was an excellent teacher—a super teacher. He was very tolerant, but he was also demanding because he wanted it done to perfection; that's the way he did it himself. I think *Kung Fu* came much out of what was seen just on the one show of *Longstreet*, and it became a very big thing. The martial arts were a big thing before they were in films here. And their popularity is certainly evidenced in his films that are appearing now.

I think Bruce was a martial artist first and an actor second—no question about that. I have never seen anyone who could control his own destiny in a physical sense as much as Bruce was able to. But he also had a great sense of humor, and it struck me that . . . I guess he was like the great football players. Thank God they are gentle people! He had the capacity to kill you with one blow, but he was just the opposite kind of a fellow. Here was a man who was a walking machete and yet, as an individual, was as gentle a man, as tolerant and unassuming, as I have ever known.

Chapter 13

Bruce Lee as Seen Through the Eyes of Students of Jeet Kune Do

DAN INOSANTO

My relationship with Bruce was as a friend and an instructor. As a friend, I don't think I've had anyone who has helped me as much as Bruce has. As an instructor, I feel I am very fortunate to have trained under him.

Bruce taught us that jeet kune do was a means of knowing yourself physically, spiritually, and emotionally. His main theme was to seek truth and liberate ourselves. He stressed learning to depend our ourselves for expression rather than blindly following his instruction, to be creative and not bound by the principles of karate, or boxing, or wrestling. He always stressed creativity.

Bruce felt that knowledge in life and in the martial arts comes from oneself, but that it has to be awakened in you. He often said to me that I shouldn't teach, but guide. In fact, that was one of the criticisms that he had of me. He said, "Dan, you try to teach too much. This is not karate. This is not kempo. This is not kung fu. The best thing you can do for your students is to give them a feeling of success. Guide your students to find their own capabilities and their own talents. Help them grow, force them to do their own problem solving, by giving them frustration. Guide them to find the cause of their ignorance.''

This is the main thing Bruce tried to stamp into me. Give them learning experiences. Make them experience things that normally they wouldn't experience fighting only against a Japanese stylist, or a Chinese stylist, or a Korean stylist, or an Okinawan stylist.

I don't think anyone could teach as well as Bruce. He could get you emotionally involved. He didn't like to teach more than three students. In fact, in all his teachings, he never taught more than six students at one time. I think he felt that teaching could not take place if you had more than six students, that you would be drilling like a karate class, and he didn't want that. He wanted me to carry on the art in the same manner. He said, ''Only have six students, Dan.'' But we've gotten a little bit crowded, and I've had to take a little more than 12 students.

Within the jeet kune do organization, I feel there are people who are much more talented than I am, who are physically better than I am. Bruce could have picked any instructor, but he chose me. I don't know why. But I feel honored that he spent the time with me. It was just like a dream to me.

Bruce once looked at me and said, ''Ability is of no concern. A man's personality is the primary thing, the thing I choose.'' He wanted a person of good character. He wanted a person with a good moral background. He didn't have to be a perfect person because no one is really perfect. But Bruce's main concern was he didn't want the art to be like karate. He didn't want to open a commercial school. This is one of the promises that I made to him—that I would never open up a commercial school under the name jeet kune do. He said, ''You could probably make some money out of it. But I'd be very disappointed if you did.'' So I have always kept this in mind.

We have a class here in Los Angeles. It's a small place—30 by 40—but we screen carefully. There's a board, and if there are five votes, the member goes in. The board is very selective nowadays. The older members got together recently and wanted me to really tighten up. I have a vote, but the other ten do also, and usually five to eight votes will get you in.

I recall that Bruce reacted indifferently to the fame he received. He really didn't think too much of it. He used to talk about it, but I think he was very humble. I know you'll hear conflicting stories that he was cocky, but it was a kind of cockiness that came from experience and confidence. He was such a perfectionist that sometimes he would lose his patience with himself and me. That was the only fault he had, if you could call it a fault. But in the long run, I found out that it really helped me.

When Bruce was in Northern California, he taught a little of his method

Bruce Lee's exceptional physique can be seen in this still from Enter the Dragon.

to some black belts, and they turned around and added it to their system This really upset him. By the time he came to Los Angeles and founded the idea of jeet kune do, he was very reserved about completely showing his method to others. But if you take Bruce Lee's stuff, you can take any style and make it better—because it gives you a set of principles to follow. I could go back and open a kenpo school, and just by flowering it up with jeet kune do a little bit, I could make my kenpo much more functional. Dan Lee has made his tai chi and his boxing functional from having known Bruce. I understand my *escrima* (a Filipino form of combat using sticks, clubs, short saber, swords, lance, and empty hands) much better because of Bruce. By using his principles and following his creative methods, Bruce could perform escrima even though he had no formal training in it.

Bruce was creative and original. He advanced in the martial arts because he dared to question the principles that were laid as rules, or foundations. Bruce said, "There is no rule that has been set down that cannot be broken. It might have been functional at one time, but it may not be functional today." He didn't believe in things like ippon kumite, one-stage free-styling, or three-stage sparring, as they refer to it. He felt it was dead; not alive. And even in his basics, he tried to make things alive. He said, "A drill has to be functional. It has to be close to the reality." If it was not, he would throw it out.

I've tried to follow this concept even in my physical education teaching. If a drill never occurs in a game situation or in a real-life situation, why do it? You're never practicing it the way you would practice in a game situation. Reverting back to martial arts, I feel you should take all of these martial arts drills and make them functional. Of course, there are drills that make you stronger, faster, give you better agility—things like that. Well, that's different, for a different purpose. As far as the fighting skill drills are concerned, they must be closer to reality. In other words, it's useless if a guy comes in with a lunge punch and you learn 100 techniques for a lunge punch, or what they call a step-through punch. Very few people walk in like that except for a karateman.

"Come in like a boxer would come in," Bruce used to say. "Come in swinging like a streetfighter would swing." And that's the way we practice in jeet kune do. It might look formless, and when I first looked at his training methods, I said "What is this?" because I had already had some preconceived ideas of what a martial artist should look like, what type of form he should have. I thought his foot should be flat, his body should be this way, etc. And every style has this preconceived idea of what a good martial artist *should* look like, and that has nothing to do with it, as Bruce always tried to point out. It took me six months to understand this principle.

Bruce dared to question things. He said to me, "Dan, if it doesn't work for you, throw it away. But you should drill on it first. Know the rules, follow the rules, dissolve the rules." He had three stages.

I have a letter from Bruce, dated December 28, 1965, when he was living in Seattle, Washington, in which he wrote, ". . . the International Karate Championship uses my three stages of cultivation of kung fu in its international karate emblem. The first stage is the primitive stage. It is a stage of original ignorance in which a person knows nothing about the art of combat. In a fight, he simply blocks and strikes instinctively without a concern as to what is right and wrong. Of course, he may not be so-called scientific, but, nevertheless, being himself, his attacks or defenses are fluid.

"The second stage—the stage of sophistication, or mechanical stage—begin when a person starts his training. He is taught the different ways of blocking, striking, kicking, standing, breathing, and thinking. Unquestionably, he has gained the scientific knowledge of combat, but unfortunately his original self and sense of freedom are lost, and his action no longer flows by itself. His mind tends to freeze at different movements for calculations and analysis, and, even worse, he might be called 'intellectually bound' and maintain himself outside the actual reality.

"The third stage—the stage of alertness, or spontaneous stage—occurs when, after years of serious and hard practice, he realizes that, after all, kung fu is nothing special. And instead of trying to impose on his mind, he adjusts himself to his opponent like water pressing on an earthen wall. It flows through the slight crack. There is nothing to try to do but to be purposeless and formless, like water. All of his classical techniques and standard styles are minimized, if not wiped out, and nothingness prevails. He is no longer confined.

"Dan, forget about fancy horses, of moving the horse, fancy forms, pressure, locking, etc. All these will promote your mechanical aspects rather than help you. You will be bound by these unnatural rhythmic messes, and when you are in combat it is broken rhythm and timing you have to adjust to. The opponent is not going to do things rhythmically with you as you would do in practicing a kata alone or with a partner. . . ."

Bruce gave me confidence. I was kind of shy, bashful, and I think he helped my personality in that respect, that he taught me to be confident and more outgoing. He asked me, "Why are you bashful? Have you ever thought of that, Dan?" And I said, "Well, I guess I'm scared of people." He asked, "Why are you scared of people?" and I answered, "Well, I'm scared of making mistakes." He came back with, "What could happen to you if you did make a mistake in public?" And I then listed the things that could happen—the worst things that could possibly happen. I guess he used the Socratic method because he would never answer for me. He would always let me answer.

This was Bruce's way of teaching, also. Instead of having you do 500 kicks, he would get you emotionally involved in ten kicks. He would always ask questions during training to get you to seek the truth about yourself. Usually when a person is philosophical in his teaching, it doesn't apply to his training. But with Bruce, I found it was just the opposite. He used to tell me that any technique, no matter how worthy and desirable, becomes a disease when your mind becomes obsessed with it, when it is just one aspect of it. So basically, that was his philosophy: learn the principle, abide by the principle, and dissolve the principle. Obey the principle without being bound to it. And basically that's jeet kune do.

Bruce was a beautiful person. He was ahead of his time in the martial arts, and sometimes people just didn't understand what he was trying to convey. I feel he was the Einstein or the Edison of the martial arts, and some people in the arts just weren't ready for him. I must agree with Leo Fong (a kung fu karate instructor in Stockton, California), who said Bruce Lee was like the seagull in the book *Jonathan Livingston Seagull.* I truly feel Bruce was the Jonathan Livingston Seagull of martial arts.

DAN LEE

The first time I saw Bruce was in 1964 at a demonstration in Long Beach. I was impressed with his speed, his power, and his insight into martial arts. I had studied kempo karate for four years with Danny Inosanto, and I knew he was studying with Bruce, but I didn't have the opportunity to study with him until some time later.

In 1967, I received a call from Danny telling me that Bruce was going to start a jeet kune do school in Los Angeles and that he would recommend me to Bruce if I was interested. I was overjoyed!

As far as choosing a student was concerned, I think Bruce considered a person's sincerity in learning and willingness to train hard the two most important prerequisites. In fact, every student training in his school was on probation for six months. Not until you had proven your sincerity and showed marked improvement from your persistent training did he admit you as a full member of his school. One thing I treasure most is becoming the first permanent member of his Los Angeles school.

Bruce accepted both beginners and those with previous training, but I think he preferred someone that already had some martial art background. A beginner probably wouldn't really understand what Bruce had to say. I think a student would have to have gone through all that formal training in order to appreciate the simplicity of what Bruce had to offer.

During the first few months of training, Bruce stressed the importance of physical conditioning: fitness, flexibility exercises, and basic punching and kicking drills. We trained four times a week, and they were always grueling sessions. As a result, quite a few quit after a few weeks. I think that in a way Bruce was testing our sincerity and willingness to train hard. The fitness program finally eased off at the fourth month, and he began to train those who remained.

Bruce was revolutionary in his approach, creating new training methods and devices. He did not believe in fixed stances or prearranged and complicated techniques. He believed in direct, simple, and effective techniques. To him, punching and kicking were our basic tools, and we were drilled in different ways in order to sharpen and perfect these tools.

Bruce said to us, "Look at any tool as an art. Remember, for a single tool to be a masterpiece, it must have totality, speed, agility, power, flexibility, and accuracy. Until you have the ability to move your body and adapt to whatever the object happens to be in front of you, as well as punch and kick from any angle, you still haven't gotten your total efficiency."

Bruce was a great teacher. His philosophical approach toward martial art and his illustrations were unique and refreshing. Whenever he explained the philosophy of a technique, he would demonstrate with his lightning-fast movements. I could not believe the explosive power he could generate in his punches and kicks. He must have spent countless hours perfecting them.

Training under Bruce was a continuous enlightening experience. Even in group training, he observed each student carefully and pointed out specific areas each must work on. Our progress was carefully tested and recorded. I remember one day he passed a sheet to each student. To my surprise, they were all different. Based on his observations, he had personally typed a supplementary training program for each of us. I really treasure that personal touch and the thoroughness of Bruce's teaching. To this day, I still use my personal supplementary training program.

In his JKD philosophy, Bruce stressed simplicity in approach and the direct expression of one's inner feelings. That is, in essence, Bruce Lee. There was no artificiality in him. He was honest in his feelings and said exactly what was in his mind. He had a child-like pureness in this modern, complex society. When he moved to Culver City, and later to Bel-Air, we all gladly helped him move. Bruce was very appreciative of our efforts, but he never took advantage of us because he was our *sifu* (teacher).

Bruce was fair and straightforward. I remember in one of the early sessions, when he was testing each student's flexibility in bag kicking, one student was having a hard time raising his leg. While he was struggling at the

In The Chinese Connection, *Bruce took on and defeated an entire school.*

bag, another student giggled. Bruce turned around, looked at him with those piercing eyes, and said coldly, "I want you to wipe that smile off your face right this minute or get out of this class!"

There was a time when I visited him every weekend and trained at his home with a few other students. While we were training, there was total seriousness. When the training was over, however, Bruce became a very close friend to us. He would share his humor and jokes, and there was always laughs and good conversation.

Bruce lived a life that was true and honest to himself and to his ideals. He mentioned once to us that money wasn't everything to him. He would rather starve than compromise his principles by portraying some ridiculous stereotype Chinese using "ah-so" in the dialogue and bouncing around with a pigtail.

There is no one teacher that has made so great an impact on my training. Bruce liberated me from the classical training of blindly following fixed routines and believing that they represent the whole truth. He re-oriented my learning attitude and helped me understand that I should place my emphasis on the essence and spirit behind these movements, rather than vainly repeating form without any feeling. He left us suddenly, and yet his ideals, his philosophy, and his insight shall remain fresh and alive in my mind forever. The totality and freedom of expression toward the ultimate reality in combat, and adapting to that ever-changing reality, shall continually be my training goal.

With Dan Inosanto's able leadership, Bruce Lee's JKD will move on. Like a new plant, it shall grow and mature, blooming with fresh flower and bearing new fruit.

Chapter 14

Bruce Lee as Seen Through the Eyes of Fellow Martial Artists

CHUCK NORRIS

The first time I met Bruce was in New York in 1967, when I was fighting Joe Lewis for the grand championship title at the All-American Karate Championship. Bruce was there as a guest of the show. After I won, I walked over to him and introduced myself. We started talking. After the tournament, around 11:00 p.m., we discovered we were in the same hotel, so we went back together. We went up to his room and until seven o'clock the next morning talked about philosophies and techniques. For eight hours, we worked out and exchanged ideas and so forth. That is where I really got to know Bruce as a martial artist.

Before that night, I hadn't known Bruce, and as a rule I don't make opinions of people until I know them. I had heard that he was very cocky and that he downgraded the other arts. But Bruce was very friendly to me. He didn't try to prove he was better than me, and he didn't downgrade any style. He just gave me his opinions of what he thought about the different arts. After talking to him, I knew he was a very knowledgeable person in the martial arts. For me to have spent eight hours with somebody and have it

The friendship between Bruce Lee and Chuck Norris predates Bruce's success in films and television. When putting together Way of the Dragon, *Bruce called on his old friend to play his most formidable opponent.*

seem like only 20 minutes had gone by, he would have to have been a very knowledgeable person—both mentally and physically.

At the time, Bruce didn't believe much in high kicking. He did a lot of kicking, but he preferred to kick from the waist down—not any higher. And, naturally, I gave him my philosophies—to be able to kick anywhere, head on down.

After I returned to Los Angeles, we started working out together at his house. I started learning his Chinese style, and he started picking up our kicks and so on.

One time I was out in Bruce's garage, and he had this dummy of a man and he said, "Kick the guy. Kick it in the head." I said, "Well, I don't know. My pants are pretty tight." (This was before they had double knit.) But he talked me into it, and I threw a high kick. I ripped the pants in the crotch all the way up the back and my pants fell down to my ankles. Just as I pulled them up, Linda walked in, and I had to go home hanging onto my pants. I haven't worn anything but double knit since then!

Bruce was a very "ego" guy. He was very confident of his ability and knowledge, and, in turn, he stated it to people. Some people didn't like that; they don't like for you to say how good you are, and Bruce was the type that would say how good he was. To me, that wasn't bad. It was just his whole personality.

Whether it was true or not, I felt that Bruce, being small, wanted to be, pound for pound, the strongest man in the world. And I think he was.

Bruce was not the easiest person to read. But working out with him, exchanging philosophies and so forth, I could see that he was always striving to learn. He was very creative. He was a genius at creating new ideas. This is what amazed me about him—his inventions, the new things he would create and develop. When he started working on some type of apparatus, he wouldn't stop until he became an expert at it. Like the Devlin ball, kicking the bag, and things like that. He wouldn't give up on something until he was extremely proficient in that one specific area.

Bruce Lee's style fit Bruce Lee. No other human being had ever trained the way Bruce trained—fanatically. He lived and breathed it from the time he got up at six o'clock in the morning until he went to bed at night. He was either working out or thinking about it. His mind was always active; never resting. He was always thinking about what he could do to improve himself or what new inventions were possible. His mind was constantly active.

With his role as Kato in *The Green Hornet* series, Bruce was the forerunner for really exploding the martial arts to its popularity. It's a shame a great martial artist such as Bruce had to leave us so soon, but I feel that he accomplished more in his lifetime than most people will accomplish in 70 or 80 years, so I don't feel that he was really shortchanged. He really accomplished what he wanted in life, and that is what life is about. It is not how long you live but what you accomplish while you are living. I feel that Bruce accomplished the goal that he wanted; he was a well-known actor, acclaimed for his martial arts ability. I think he lived a full life.

WALLY JAY

My first association with Bruce was in Seattle, Washington, in 1962. We met in the basement of a Chinese church where he was teaching wing chun. Bruce explained the theory of his kung fu while demonstrating. His *chi sao* (sticky hands) ability fascinated me, and his wide knowledge of the art at the young age of 22 amazed me.

While in college, I taught boxing. I have always told my pupils that you sacrifice punching power if you want speed. Bruce's demonstration of lightning speed blows which still maintained the devastating punching power of a

A group portrait shows the members of Bruce Lee's kwoon in Los Angeles·

heavyweight blew up my theory. He also used beautiful wrist action in his moves, which I believe is the little thing that success depends on. I was convinced this young man knew a lot.

Bruce was interested in all martial arts. I found jujitsu books in his library at his home in Los Angeles, and he demonstrated judo throws at my dojo. He boxed in Hong Kong, but he didn't like the gloves. He needed his fingers and hands to feel with. Bruce was intelligent and captivated his audience with his fluid moves and sound theory. He could expound on it for hours and still not bore anyone with his wide, varied knowledge. He did step on many toes when he criticized the teaching of non-essential moves by various systems. But all of his critics are enjoying his success with their larger classes today.

Bruce won a large following from the days of *The Green Hornet.* In my town—Alameda, California—Kato was the hero of all the children. A few months ago, several of Bruce's admirers came to visit my dojo. They had found out that Bruce was my personal friend, and they just wanted to shake hands with me. They said this would be the closest they would ever get to Bruce Lee, their idol. They loved him.

Bruce showed me great respect and often wanted to hear of my success. In his letters, he would send words of encouragement and inspiration. He appeared on stage at several of my club's benefit luaus, and although I paid his airfare from Seattle or Los Angeles, he would not accept any monetary compensation for his appearances. Bruce always said, "It is a benefit for Island Judo Club, and I only want my airfare paid."

Bruce had a dynamic personality. He was a great showman. But in all my discussions with him, I felt there was something about him that I could not place. One day, Bruce, Jimmy Lee, and Linda (Bruce's wife) visited me at my home. We discussed Bruce's ability to punch with blinding speed and yet maintain devastating punching power. He explained the theory to me and then asked Linda to demonstrate it to me. He said that she had had about six months of instruction, and her exhibition won my approval. But before I could give my reply, Bruce cracked a handsome boyish smile, acknowledging my acceptance. He had read my facial expression. He turned to Linda, looking into her eyes, and smiled to let her know she had impressed me.

This smile of approval or acknowledgement was Bruce's facial trademark. I have seen it so often in his motion pictures. That smile left me a lasting impression of the creative, innovative, and daring Bruce Lee.

Bruce was a dear friend and I miss him. There will never be another Bruce Lee—so knowledgeable, sincere, and kind. Someone said that Bruce was a hundred years beyond our time. I agree. He was my shining light. That Bruce Lee was something—something special.

BOB WALL

Bruce gave me my start as far as films are concerned. He had a brilliant martial arts mind, and he gave me a lot of insight into the martial arts. He did not want to prostitute his art, but he wanted to express it to the world. He taught me that there was a much more honest way of expressing your art than, let's say, through sport karate (sparring and tournaments) because he felt there was no "true" winner on a point system. At any rate, he really made me think about my martial art philosophy.

I would say one of the most important things I learned from Bruce was the fact that although he was an extremely tough man, he was a very, very sensitive one. Several situations showed that he didn't want to hurt anybody. He cornered some of the people that forced him into physical confrontations, yet he wouldn't hurt anybody. He would just kind of show them that he could play with them and yet not hurt them.

Normally, Bruce shunned challenges, but one time in Hong Kong a kid challenged him. He was sitting on a wall, and he cursed Bruce in Chinese (I had to get this second hand about what was said. I heard the Chinese, but I didn't understand it.) He told Bruce that he was a phony, that he was just a "movie" karateman, and that he wasn't really a good martial artist.

We were in between takes, so Bruce said, "C'mon down and beat me up!" The kid jumped down and really started trying to take Bruce out. This kid was good. He was no punk. He was strong and fast, and he was really trying to punch Bruce's brains in. But Bruce just methodically took him apart. He slammed the kid into a rock wall, then trapped him with his right knee and left hand. He took the kid's hand, punched in, just touched his cheek, brought his hand back, and said, "See, you're mine." He had the kid locked up! He couldn't move. He bloodied his mouth, got him up, and rammed him into that wall about three more times just to show him that he could have him against that wall anytime he wanted. He made the kid fight until he couldn't move a muscle, and then he talked to him and said, "This is a lesson for you. I want you to understand." Bruce was doing it like a lesson! He told him, "Look, your stance is too wide; you were doing this." And then the kid shook his hands and said, "You really are a master of the martial arts," and he climbed back up on the wall.

It was the first time I had seen Bruce truly mad because this kid was swinging to punch is head off. At first, I think Bruce thought the kid was just kind of jesting, but this kid hated him. He wanted to punch his brains out. But when it was over, Bruce was his hero. Bruce humiliated the kid for doing something that was really wrong, and yet he learned a lot about his martial art. Bruce not only punched the kid out, but he didn't hurt him doing it. I was very impressed.

Bruce was superbly prepared; kind of like Muhammad Ali in his heyday or Bobby Fisher, who knew he would win when he got to Iceland. As long as he didn't get cheated, he knew there was no way for him to lose. And it's really like any good businessman or any knowledgeable person. If you're properly prepared, you know that you put all the odds in your favor.

First of all, Bruce was prepared because he studied acting. He studied techniques, the camera, and so forth. I think the most important thing was his confidence and intellectual capacity. He was a very smart man. Most people are confident exteriorly, but interiorly they are not. And I think one of Bruce's secrets was that he felt he had not anywhere passed his potential. He knew he had weaknesses. He was a mortal; a human being. So he was continually working to not be a little, teeny, skinny runt Chinese. He really broke all the ethnic barriers. He thought of himself as a man—an extremely

In this still from Chinese Connection, *Bruce strikes a bodybuilder's pose.*

powerful and bright man.

Bruce was a searcher. He was always looking to improve himself in any way. Nutritionally, he had a good diet; physically, he had a good exercise program; and psychologically, he was always looking for ways to improve his mind and his ability to communicate with people. I think that was probably his strength: the fact that he was pretty well-rounded.

Bruce was the first good martial artist to ever get on the screen. And once you have somebody really good, it forces everybody else to get better. For years, the martial artists that did get on TV were not professional martial artists. They just claimed to be, and they made a bad impression. It's like anything else. The screen is bigger than life. It magnifies either your good or your bad points.

Bruce was the first good one to deal in the martial arts. He demonstrated that there is a tremendous audience for martial arts. I don't think his films were necessarily inordinately violent. For the most part, there was no unnecessary killing. So, I think he paved the way for martial artists to take over where the Westerns left off. Westerns have always been popular because they are probably the last masculine frontier. I feel that martial art is a new masculine frontier. People respect a man who is deadly, tough, and, yet, not a bully. These are the things I think Bruce opened up, merged with the fact that you can't go in and fake martial arts. You have got to use a real martial artist. Bruce was great, and people could see it on film because he was bigger than life up there.

Bruce was a very demanding person to work with. He wanted what he wanted, and he wanted it right then. He would lay things down at your doorstep, so to speak, and expect you to pick them up. And, yet, he had patience if he felt you were giving 110 percent; then he would work with you all the way. He wouldn't abruptly interfere, but he was a little tough if you wanted to make suggestions: he didn't want to hear them. I guess he felt he was thinking way beyond you. So it was very difficult to really participate in creating something, although once in a while you could. But it was always exciting to work with him because he was always teaching you something. Maybe you'd be busy trying to learn how to take a punch or a kick or something, and you wouldn't be paying attention to the camera. He'd say, "Look, there are so many things to observe. Don't just get hung up on one thing." He was always spouting philosophy, and he was stimulating.

Once Bruce taught me how to take a punch on screen. He said, "OK, I'm

Bob Wall plays an especially skilled karate man in Way of the Dragon. *He is hired to finish off Bruce Lee's character but is instead done in by Lee.*

Bob Wall takes Bruce's side kick in the stomach in Way of the Dragon.

going to throw a punch. I want you to react to it.'' When he threw the punch, I turned my shoulders and my head and my neck stiff because I had never thought about it. This is something most people have never thought about. I've never seen anyone do it naturally. It's just a very unnatural movement—to pretend you've just been hit violently and to time it. Bruce taught me how to relax my body, how to bend my knees and get up on my toes a little bit. He said, ''Imagine you're being hit. Think about it. What does it feel like? *Feel* it. Feel what you're doing.'' He had me relax and stand in front of a mirror and snap my head until my neck was so sore I could hardly whip it for a week.

Bruce was not perfect. Like all of us, he had his flaws. But anybody who knew him respected him because he was a brilliant person. He was a nice man. He was really a rare human being. I don't think there will ever be another Bruce Lee. He was a very individual person. I feel very fortunate that I got to know him, and I am thrilled that I got to work with him. I am very saddened that he is gone; yet I'm happy he was here. It wouldn't have been such a great loss if he hadn't been here to start with. So I'm glad that he at least got the opportunity to pave the way for the rest of us.

MIKE STONE

I think I am one of maybe four or five people who had the pleasure of working with Bruce in his home. I went to his house once a week. Wednesdays were normally my day to work out with him. In a way, it was really an exchange of ideas more than a student-instructor relationship. There were a lot of things I wanted to pick up to improve my sparring ability, such as his attitude of simplicity in self-defense.

Bruce was a clown. He used to cut up a lot. He was always the center of attraction, just like a kid as far as his enthusiasm and bubbly personality were concerned. He was always clowning around and cracking jokes and just keeping everybody in good spirits. He was great that way.

For his size and weight, Bruce was one of the strongest people—pound for pound—I have ever met. I think he could have beaten a lot of people much heavier and much stronger than he was. He would have done extremely well in competition; if anything, he would have been much too fast for a lot of the officials. He was that skillful.

I think Bruce would have done extremely well in a streetfighting situation because of one quality that he had: the desire to succeed and to win. Of course, Bruce had a lot of other things that were necessary, too. He had the talent and he had the knowledge. A lot of people have as strong a desire to succeed, but without the knowledge, the proper working of that knowledge, and the ability, you just can't succeed. Bruce was gifted in a way that he had a tremendous amount of outstanding qualities just wrapped up in one person. And they all added to him getting his success so much faster than most people would. I think Bruce accomplished in three or four years what would normally take someone else a lifetime—25, 30 years—to accomplish.

One of Bruce's strongest characteristics was his belief in himself, in his ability, and his talent. He was a very intelligent person; not just physically talented and intelligent, but mentally intelligent. I think he expected a lot out of people because he demanded a lot of himself. He was that way—a perfectionist in his abilities.

Bruce had a tremendous amount to offer. He was one of the most knowledgeable martial arts people I have ever met, but he was a little bit more advanced than his time. A lot of people probably could not understand his theory because it was so simple. For the most part, people come into the martial arts expecting so much. They think there is a secret potion that is taken in order to gain this ability and knowledge. And then they realize it is just basically hard work and a matter of perfecting simplicity. This is what Bruce advocated, and a lot of people thought it sounded way too simple to be logical and realistic.

I think Bruce has done more for karate in the United States in a shorter time than all of the people put together since the first commercial studio opened up here. He had a tremendous amount of exposure, but he did it in such a way that he lifted the image and ability of what a karate person is. And his quality and ability showed in his work. I think he was a great asset to the martial arts.

JHOON RHEE

I had known Bruce ever since the 1964 International Karate Championships, where we presented our demonstrations. Since then, we had become such good friends that we exchanged house visits with our families from time to time. We all felt fortunate to have such a close relationship with a man who was so genuinely great in the martial arts field and who in real life was a very kind, warm-hearted and true human being. Really, I have never met anybody who was more dedicated to the martial arts than Bruce. If you could have seen his home, you would have seen nothing but martial arts books and a gararge full of training equipment.

I remember in 1968: Bruce was off the air in the TV series *The Green Hornet* and he was having some financial problems. I know many people were approaching him to start "Kato Karate Schools" throughout the country. But in his mind, that was completely out of the question. Sometimes he would say, "To hell with these circumstances! *I* will make the circumstances from now on!" He also told me, "Jhoon, within five years, I am going to make myself the biggest and highest recognized actor as well as martial art-

A rare shot captures two greats, Bruce Lee and Jhoon Rhee, in action.

ist.'' He would never yield from his basic belief, even though he had such strong financial obligations facing him. If anyone ever showed his confidence, Bruce sure did.

Bruce worked very, very hard and had exactly what it took to make himself famous. More and more I am beginning to believe he was *gifted* with the coordination, speed, and power that he had. Notedly, he was a very skillful martial artist. Secondly, he was a man of confidence. Bruce had so much confidence in himself and life that he developed philosophical thoughts that equipped him to make it—both mentally and physically.

Whenever Bruce visited my home, or I his home, we would stay up until four o'clock in the morning, punching and kicking. He had such a sense of humor that he constantly cracked jokes. He was a jovial person. I have always said to my wife and friends that he was just like a seven-year-old boy— energetic, ran around all day.

When we were working out at my house, my wife would fix food for us whenever we got hungry. Bruce liked *sushi* very much and Korean foods. Immediately afterward, we would continue to bounce each other around. We really had great times together. In fact, I think I was the last guy from the United States to see him in Hong Kong before he died because I had just finished a film called *When Tae Kwon Do Strikes*. Sometimes Bruce would wait on the set until I finished, and then we'd go to dinner.

I will do my best to honor Bruce's dedication and his contribution to the martial arts. If ever a dream came true, I'd like most of all to see his birthday —November 27—be set aside as a "Day of Martial Arts." It would be a great tribute to him and his followers.

More Bruce Lee Books from Ohara

TAO OF JEET KUNE DO
by Bruce Lee. Code No. 401

BRUCE LEE'S FIGHTING METHOD Vol. 1: Self-Defense Techniques
by Bruce Lee and M. Uyehara. Code No. 402

BRUCE LEE'S FIGHTING METHOD Vol. 2: Basic Training
by Bruce Lee and M. Uyehara. Code No. 403

BRUCE LEE'S FIGHTING METHOD Vol. 3: Skill in Techniques
by Bruce Lee and M. Uyehara. Code No. 404

BRUCE LEE'S FIGHTING METHOD Vol. 4: Advanced Techniques
by Bruce Lee and M. Uyehara. Code No. 405

CHINESE GUNG FU
by Bruce Lee. Code No. 451

THE LEGENDARY BRUCE LEE
by the Editors of Black Belt magazine. *Code No. 446*

THE BRUCE LEE STORY
by Linda Lee. Code No. 460

THE INCOMPARABLE FIGHTER
by M. Uyehara. Code No. 461

OHARA ▯ **PUBLICATIONS, INC.,** 24715 Ave. Rockefeller, P.O. Box 918, Santa Clarita, CA 91380-9018